Area

Unveiling the Enigma of Area 51
(Unraveling Secrets in the Shadows of America's Most Secure Zone)

Damian Ojeda

Published By **Ryan Princeton**

Damian Ojeda

All Rights Reserved

*Area 51: Unveiling the Enigma of Area 51
(Unraveling Secrets in the Shadows of America's
Most Secure Zone)*

ISBN 978-1-7782825-2-2

No part of this guidebook shall be reproduced in any form without permission in writing from the publisher except in the case of brief quotations embodied in critical articles or reviews.

Legal & Disclaimer

The information contained in this book is not designed to replace or take the place of any form of medicine or professional medical advice. The information in this book has been provided for educational & entertainment purposes only.

The information contained in this book has been compiled from sources deemed reliable, and it is accurate to the best of the Author's knowledge; however, the Author cannot guarantee its accuracy and validity and cannot be held liable for any errors or omissions. Changes are periodically made to this book. You must consult your doctor or get professional medical advice before using any of the suggested remedies, techniques, or information in this book.

Upon using the information contained in this book, you agree to hold harmless the Author from and against any damages, costs, and expenses, including any legal fees potentially resulting from the application of any of the information provided by this guide. This disclaimer applies to any damages or injury caused by the use and application, whether directly or indirectly, of any advice or information presented, whether for breach of contract, tort, negligence, personal injury, criminal intent, or under any other cause of action.

You agree to accept all risks of using the information presented inside this book. You need to consult a professional medical practitioner in order to ensure you are both able and healthy enough to participate in this program.

Table Of Contents

Chapter 1: The Land of Dreams 1

Chapter 2: The Conspiracy Begin 16

Chapter 3: There's a possibility 32

Chapter 4: Which Base Is It? 55

Chapter 5: What is the level of security in the area 51? 83

Chapter 6: The beginnings of Disclosure or Misinformation? 102

Chapter 7: Tacit Blue 116

Chapter 8: A New Beginning 129

Chapter 9: Initial News Reports 139

Chapter 10: The Majestic 12 155

Chapter 11: Kingsman UFO Amazing Trail 167

Chapter 12: Cape Girardeau from the Condon Report 182

Chapter 1: The Land of Dreams

In spite of its lengthy, filled with rumors of bizarre comings and goings Area 51 didn't officially exist until 2013. The year in which the CIA breathed a sigh of relief as it declassified documents and finally revealed what everybody else already knew: there was an undiscovered base within the region of the Nevada desert that is known by the name of Area 51. But this acknowledgement of the existence of a base only went all the way that the agency would go. The agency has yet to provide an answer to the ever-growing conspiratorial theories and speculation on what is actually happening in the area.

A lot of people have thought for a long time that this bizarre military camp in the desert could be a sort of oasis in the supernatural in which aliens and human beings interacted on about technology as well as clandestine research and anything else that caught their interests. It was the case with David Adair, who as a young rocket engineer was said to be shown a gigantic UFO "motor" also known as a propulsion device pulled from an UFO that he claimed was "alive."

The most famous story was that involved Bob Lazar, who claimed to have been involved in the development of such propulsion systems prior to being excluded from the program but still survived to tell his story. A microbiologist was also a part of the program who claimed that he had encountered an extraterrestrial being who was a part of the Area 51 residents dressed with casual clothing for men and called "J-Rod."

These are the unforgettable stories of UFO stories that have spawned many documentary and book. And now the fact that Area 51 is finally accepted as a genuine physical place what does it translate to these unbelievable tales? Does it give credence to these stories or do they completely discredit the claims?

Area 51 is often called by fans and even supposed insiders by the name of "Dreamland," apparently in an homage to the fantastical and dreamlike nature of what happens in the area. Many who visit it experience the sensation of entering an entirely new world. With the recent revelations possibly, Dreamland is only just awakening to potential.

It was the Early Days of Area 51

The area that is Southern Nevada that Area 51 has chosen to call home is an unhospitable desert. Prior to the time that it was the time that U.S. military began to establish bases in the area in the early 1990s, it was essentially inaccessible to the public. There were only a few scattered Native American tribes such as the Paiute and Shoshone tried to make some sort of existence within the tiny places of greenery hidden among the vast tracts in desert sand.

The extreme isolation of the area was an important reason why the military selected the site to conduct nuclear tests and exercise using top-secret aircraft. They desired an isolated location, as away from the prying eyes of anyone as they could, and the region of desert that which was later named Area 51 fit that description perfect.

The first time that the military was involved in the area dates from the month of October, 1940. The time was when the president Franklin Delano Roosevelt signed an executive decree transferring 3 million acres of this Nevada desert area to the United States Army Air Corps. The USAAC initially referred to the large portion of land that was outside Las Vegas as the "Las Vegas Bombing and Gunnery Range." It served as a perfect place to train in the years prior to World War Two.

Following the war, following the creation of the first world nuclear bombs in the year 1945, they United States Atomic Energy Commission acquired a significant portion of what was later to become Area 51 for nuclear testing. This area was known as "Nevada Proving Grounds" or, more commonly, in the "Nevada Testing Site." It was not surprising that as the people from Las Vegas first received word of nukes dropped "somewhere" within their huge desert landscape there was a little reservations about the plan.

After the AEC began directing the funds needed to build projects close to Las Vegas, much of worry faded away to background. A few residents even participated in events at the site of testing by hosting "viewing gatherings," which consisted of outdoor barbecues where guests were able to look out to the horizon in case a distant cloud from an atomic bomb blast was visible emerging somewhere in the distant desert.

The program was said to be kept secret but the smoke gun in the cloud of mushroom ashes left nothing for the imagination. It was obvious for anyone who was casually watching that nuclear tests were taking place throughout Southwest Nevada. This is why in addition to the Nuclear Test Ban Treaty of 1963, the tests were eventually relocated underground, placing the brakes on viewing events to the fullest extent.

It was during the time that the AEC was in the middle of testing nuclear weapons that the newly-established United States Air Force first utilized the area of desert real estate that was later referred to by the name of Area 51. The AEC employed grids to identify specific areas of land using the terms areas 1,2 3... as well etc. It is widely thought that the name Area 51 originates from this system of classification.

It's also interesting to consider that the grounds of Area 51 are located directly adjacent to the previous AEC testing ground, which was designated Area 15. Some have even believe there was a possibility that they Air Force simply inverted the numbers in order to have their own part in the pie of desert.

However, it was in the area of the dry bed in Groom Lake that the Air Force as well as the CIA began to established their own the shop. The location was also where they launched Project Aquatone.

The saying goes necessity is the source of invention. This definitely was the case in Project Aquatone. In the years when Cold War tensions between the United States and the Soviet Union were at a peak and it was decided by it was time that the U.S. Air Force needed an active method of surveillance against their Communist adversaries. The military strategists were aware that any aircraft found spying on Soviet airspace could be destroyed, leading to a further escalation of tension and even the possibility of war.

For this purpose that U.S. was looking for an improved, more modern plane that could be able to fly at such an altitude that it would be practically undetectable in the

1950s Soviet radars on ground. Project Aquatone was designed to create such a flying vehicle which was the end product of their efforts is the U-2 spy aircraft. It was developed for a maximum of 70,700 feet in altitude -- into the atmosphere's upper levels--so it could carry out secret flyovers in and over the Soviet Union with impunity.

The prototype first made its maiden flight in the month of the month of August in 1955. Since the beginning that time, the CIA was given a distinct task in the development by training its agents to pilot the craft. It was for the defensibility factor that came with the presence of an CIA officer dressed in civilian attire piloting the aircraft. Should it crashed over hostile territory and the military was able to claim that they were not conscious of or accountable for the flight. It could be put on the shoulders of a civilian entity (whatever civilian organization the CIA could come up with for to cover) who simply went out of its way and strayed from its boundaries.

A lot of these planes were equipped with NACA (National advisory committee for Aeronautics, the precursor of NASA) symbols for the purpose of ensuring that, should they be caught in the event of a capture, the CIA agent would be able to drop the claim the fact that he was just doing a research study and was taken off course. Incredibly, there was a noticeable increase of UFO sightings following the Project Aquatone's tests of U-2 planes started in Nevada. There is a theory that the reports were due to the sunlight reflecting off the silvery wings that spanned the length of the aircraft at higher altitudes.

In all likelihood, if you watch enough conspiracy theories, you'll find the idea that Area 51 was up to quite a bit greater than U-2 spy planes back in the 1950s early. When we talk about Area 51, it is crucial to distinguish information can be proven to be true including Project Aquatone and the U-2 as well as programs that were rumored and discussed over the years without proof.

However, as the story of Area 51 makes clear, no matter what the government says to that something isn't there does not mean they're telling us the truth. Locations such as Area 51 were built on lies and deceit, all by national security. If we believe that this justification or not, it is important to understand that just because something might seem unbelievable or out of reach does not mean it's untrue. This simply means that there isn't any evidence.

The Soviet Union's first proof of the air-flying U-2 was on May 1 60, 1960, in which they took down the the pilot Gary Powers. While the Russian aircraft was able to reach U-2's height, the spy plane faced its competition with the Russian surface-to-air missile which managed to narrow the space. The missile was launched out of Kyshtym 40, a top classified nuclear test facility that can be regarded as to be the Russian Area 51.

This mysterious building was the only thing Powers took pictures of before he heard the thunderous thud sound of the Russian SAM smashing into the aircraft, which was then which was followed by an explosive explosion that destroyed the aircraft. The remnants of the aircraft started to move forward and he realized that two of the massive wings had been torn away. When the pressure in the cabin dropped the flight suit of Powers began to expand as a balloon, making the process more and more difficult to move around as he tried to keep the plane from spinning.

Despite the force of centrifugal forces trying to hold him in place Powers was able to open the cockpit's canopy and allowed the vapors of the air to pull into the aircraft. After launching his parachute Powers took a breath of satisfaction that he'd made it through.

As he sailed towards the rolling landscape beneath the surface, his stomach began to sink in contemplating what Russians could do in the event that they came across the man. His handlers in Area 51 had told him to feed Russians -- that they were just part of a team for weather research began to appear little too unlikely.

Powers's fall was recorded at the time his feet touched the ground, the police seized him and took him straight to Moscow. He was then confined to the prison cell in which the alleged suspect was questioned repeatedly by the notorious KGB.

Then, they revealed that the Russians were already aware of Area 51. They took out an U.S. maps, laid it in front of him, and pointed his gaze towards the southwest. They kept asking Powers to explain Area 51, the "desert base" from which he'd flown from. Powers was not willing to listen to the pitch but instead of acknowledging he'd been a flight from Nevada and back to Nevada, he claimed that his base of operations was situated in the California coastline and was referred to as "Watertown."

In spite of his constant denials the charges were thrown out after just three days of trial event that was broadcast across the globe. Gary Powers was sentenced to 10 years in prison, and president Eisenhower was quite shocked by the entire incident. However, fortunately for Powers his case, the Soviets were able to reduce his sentence, and released him only two years following his arrest.

In the meantime, a U.S. government that did not wish to see any more "embarrassments" assigned Area 51 with creating an aircraft that would fly greater and more efficiently that the U-2. By combining top engineering technology with an unwavering willpower, Area 51 set out to build an aircraft that would never be destroyed by a missile.

Chapter 2: The Conspiracy Begin

There is a long-standing conspiracy theory suggesting that President Dwight Eisenhower secretly met with aliens and signed an agreement with them, referred to by the Grenada Treaty. The majority of conspiracy theorists claim that the setting of the meeting could be the Edwards Air Force base in California but in contrast to Area 51. Near but not perfect does it?

But, wait a minute. The conspiracy theories era was rekindled in 2014 after a man who claimed to be an ex-CIA agent that was placed in Area 51 put forth a entirely new version of the tale. According to him, just following the inauguration of Eisenhower, the President was reportedly hounding Area 51 for insider information regarding UFOs as well as extraterrestrials. The CIA was believed to have collected a significant amount of this information following the Roswell incident. The data was being stored at Area 51.

A recent CIA whistleblower says that when the young agent was in his first year, as well as his supervisor, they were invited to the President's office. The president informed the agents in clear phrases, "I want you and your boss to go to Washington. I'd like you to send an individual message to them and inform the person the boss, to inform that they've got a next week, which is this coming week, to travel to Washington and submit to me. If they do not, I'm going to call to the First Army of Colorado and we'll remove the base. No matter what type of classified material you've got and we'll tear the base apart!"

You can picture the flamboyant former general shouting commands like this. According an alleged former operative Ike was a serious man. He wanted to know the secrets being stored at the base in the event that he was not given the information, he'd use the power of his position and power as an ex-war hero and general to force forces into the base. However, in the end it was not enough to invade. Eisenhower believed to have agreed to let the CIA agent and his superior return to Area 51 and report back to him what they observed.

According to the rumor that occurred after reporting back to the base, the officer and his manager were transported 15 miles south of central facility located at Area 51 to a section called S4. They were then taken through massive, concealed hangers which contained a range of various saucer-type vessels that were believed to be from extraterrestrial source. The most notable of the extraterrestrial vehicles was the Roswell craft. According to the sources it was believed that all the ETs aboard the vessel had been destroyed, except for "a handful of them."

They reportedly inspected the Roswell craft from afar and went as that they tossed the craft around. It was possible since it was incredibly lightweight for its size and incredibly, it weighed less than around 150lbs. In contrast, NASA's heaviest human-powered craft was the space shuttle which weighed 165,000 pounds! If the story of a whistleblower who is supposedly leaking information is believed to be true the story is truly remarkable. Whoever designed this 150-pound spacecraft was working at a more sophisticated level of technology and production than what NASA could have imagined!

The officer goes on declare that on the fact-finding mission to Eisenhower the operative was able to watch what he called the "alien interview" where he was able to observe the questioning of an alien who was on opposite sides of a mirror with a single-way. Then they quit S4 and headed for the main base in Area 51. They were then shown the latest advancements in the what were believed to be to an extent, the effects of reverse-engineered technology from aliens: U-2, the U-2 spy plane, and the supersonic, fast and high-flying SR71 Blackbird.

The source claims that they took a flight on a commercial airline back into D.C. to report to the president Eisenhower about what they'd witnessed. Eisenhower was said to have been "shocked" by the revelations. Inquired about what the world would think of such information if it were revealed, Eisenhower requested that the veil of secret about Area 51 be clamped down to a greater extent. According to reports, it was after the debriefing,

Eisenhower's private session in person with ETs was scheduled.

In the course of the shady encounter with aliens it was thought that the president to be on holiday to Palm Springs, California, just two hours away from Edwards. The purpose was to make it one of the "working holidays" like many subsequent presidents have described the idea, but Eisenhower was required to have regular press conferences. At one of them that one of his spokesman's announcements was that Ike would not be attending in the evening.

He said that the President was able to remove the cap of one his teeth, and was escorted to an emergency treatment by the dentist. It was an bizarre and sudden announcement to people who were listening, for conspiracy theorists, it was like receiving an angelic manna. They claim that this dental issue was an elaborate cover-up; the truth is that Eisenhower was taken for Edwards Air Base to meet aliens.

Reports on what transpired following are a bit different in detail, but the essence of the matter is that Eisenhower received a brief explanation of the background of aliens as well as their motives for bringing them to Earth. Evidently, the ETs were from an era of death planet and sought assistance by way of bio-resources and land. Land part of their request was believed to have been approved by the establishment of underground bases deep in and within Area 51. The idea has been around for years that scientists from both the human and alien worlds are working in tandem in all sorts of strange tests.

For the second necessity of "biological resources" the theory is that this need could be fulfilled through the use of slaughtered cows as well as the regular abduction of a large portion from the U.S.

population. It's true: Based on this view it is believed that the Eisenhower team sold millions of Americans and agreed to allow strangers abduct them occasionally and then use their bodies as samples of genetic materials.

The ETs said that they would ensure that no one would be wounded during the procedure and that the memories associated with the experience would be erased and they'd return to the place they came from without any incident. According to reports, as a reward in exchange for U.S. cooperation in these issues, the ETs gave technological advances that were scheduled to be put into immediate application at the remote desert outpost in Area 51.

The SR-71 Blackbird and Stealth Technology

The model was known as"the SR-71 Blackbird, and for those who had the pleasure of seeing it for the first time, it was as if it came from the pages of a science-fiction novel. The swept back, sleek design, it looked much more like a space-based fighter of 100 years ago in the future, rather than an airplane from the 1960s. The Blackbird was not just able to be higher than the U-2 and reach close to 90000 feet on the limit of space. It could also travel at an incredible speed of 2200 miles per hour.

The U-2 program came to a sour final point after the spy plane controlled by Gary Powers was shot down and caused a worldwide disaster. The Blackbird did not face this problem as it flew quickly enough to beat thermal missiles. There was a sense to be impossible to catch the bird. With this new and innovative technology, Area 51 had a brand new beginning.

The SR-71 Blackbird evolved from an earlier program dubbed Archangel In which a variety of prototypes of ultra-high speed air-borne reconnaissance aircraft were classified by their degree of development, initially Archangel 1. Archangel 2. Archangel 3 Archangel 3, and finally, only by their first alphabet and number. They were then changed to A-4, A-5, and A-6 as well as A-6, etc. The most recent prototypes was called the A-12. This specific version that was the Archangel was the first to be flown from

Area 51 on April 25 of 1962. The A-12 was involved in a variety of missions, including reconnaissance efforts in Vietnam and before the successor to the SR-71 Blackbird was introduced into service in 1964.

There was no other plane similar to it in the past. The Blackbird was virtually an spacecraft, as it was able to reach the absolute boundaries of the earth's atmospheric pressure. The fact that it could reach this high altitude rendered oxygen masks that were used by other aircrafts flying at high altitudes outdated. Because of the high elevations, the Blackbird's pilots Blackbird required the full pressure suit like the ones NASA astronauts later wore for the sake of remaining alert. NASA is being developed to this day, is supposed to have learned some things through the knowledge that was gathered from the early flying tests in Area 51.

Certain conspiracists take this information one step further. They argue that the high-performance aircrafts like the Blackbird could be the start of a classified space program that was run by the CIA as a counter to NASA's. As the 1960s approached, and NASA was able to reach orbit through the rocket launches that were widely publicized The folks from Area 51 were striving to push the envelope even further by utilizing advanced planes such as the SR-71.

As impressive that the capabilities of the Blackbird were in the 1970s, there was a man who was not thrilled His name was Richard Millhouse Nixon. When Nixon was inaugurated as president, his administration aimed to cut down on what was believed was "wasteful expenditure." That included the costs of building additional SR-71 Blackbirds. Nixon declared that he did not want further Blackbirds being built. Moreover, and amazingly in addition, he ordered people in Area 51 to destroy all of the molds and assembly constructions that could have been employed to construct them.

It was a traumatic time for the many people who worked on the project. But while it was happening, the Blackbird was being moved away, Area 51 was already buzzing with the most recent in aerospace technology: it was a stealth plane. Prior to its arrival at Area 51, the stealth fighter was working for a long time. It was the Skunk Works, that is. Skunk Works Skunk Works is the name of a distinct division of the renowned aerospace manufacturer Lockheed Martin.

Led by the renowned engineering genius Ben Rich, the Skunk Works worked in the early days of stealth technologies for a long years, and they were finally rewarded with the form of a model they referred to"the "hopeless diamond." A name like that does nothing to inspire confidence, however the diamond design of the front of the prototype would make it virtually unnoticeable to radars, and according to the old saying "you cannot hit anything isn't visible," to enemy fire.

The things that did the U-2 or that of the SR-71 Blackbird did with speed and height was what the stealth fighters did with diamond shaped radar-deflecting cross-sections. The reason this model was known as"the "hopeless" diamond, was due to the fact that Skunk Works Skunk Works had had some difficulties in getting this odd designed vehicle to fly. Its diamond-shaped shape was unique with regard to its ability to block radar. It was also a struggle to get it air-like enough for flight.

The initial prototype, referred to as the "Have Blue,"" was released in the year 1976. Following their test runs at Skunk Works Skunk Works, these prototype planes were deconstructed and their components transported into Area 51 for further research and design. This was where the initial prototypes of the F-117 Stealth Fighter were made. This advancement in technology for stealth finally made its first combat test against the army of Saddam Hussein in Operation Desert Storm.

F-117s launched their first attack on Hussein's regime on the 16th of January in 1991. The Iraqi military soon realized they were unable to detect the aircraft on radars, and they decided shooting blind and straight into the air in hopes of hitting one of the F-117s with chance. The F-117s didn't get any luck however, and all of the stealth aircraft emerged to the battlefield with no scratch.

The incredible display of power and technological advancement helped quickly bring an end to the Gulf War. It is believed that it contributed to the speedy end of Cold War. It is believed that the Soviet Union, which was still on life support as of 1991, was observing the development of the Persian Gulf very carefully. The sight of this modern technology by the Americans is yet another piece of the puzzle for the dying Communist system that became completely outdated and inability to keep pace. After such impressive outcomes, it appears that the stealth plane was not a flimsy diamond in the end.

Chapter 3: There's a possibility

This chapter will take a leap from what's generally known under the light of declassified the day, and dive into the dark night of unproven conspiracy which surrounds Area 51. We discussed in detail the previous chapter of planes like the astonishingly technologically advanced SR-71 Blackbird, which we have been told was developed for the purpose of outflying Soviet interceptors.

Perhaps an aircraft such as the SR-71 Blackbird was not just intended to beat pursuers, and fend off the pursuit of its own ships. If you adhere to the standard theory, then the secretive nature of Area 51 and the mad race to design next generation aircraft such as those of the SR-71 Blackbird and the F-117 Stealth Fighter were necessitated by the growing nuclear threat posed by Russia and the Soviet Union.

In the deep and more dark world of conspiracy theories the massive research project within the Nevada desert wasn't only to design an effective plane for flights over Soviet the territory. This was also a plan to reverse engineer technology from aliens to allow competition with aliens. The idea has long been held that the reason behind the rush to build sophisticated aircrafts like those of SR-71 Blackbird and the stealth aircrafts following was a desperate effort to keep pace with the advanced alien technology that could be as large than a thousand years sophisticated.

The CIA has been reported to have used a variety of terms for coded messages used in the different phases of reverse engineering initiatives like Snowbird as well as Project Red Light. In one of the most terrifying stories, the Human technicians from Area 51 were attempting to reverse engineer the technology of UFOs. They were able to figure out the best way to propel the craft in the air, however due to some reason, it burst out during the flight and killed all aboard.

It was believed to have happened in the year 1962. It was then that the program was halted until an agreement between aliens that extraterrestrials helped human scientists figure out the best way to run the spacecraft. The outcome was Project Snowbird, and this was the time when one of the most famous and vivid people in UFO legends allegedly walked into the scene of Area 51. It was an engineer from another planet who was sent from the ETs themselves. He was known as J-Rod. (No connection to the second "J-Rod" made up from Jenifer Lopez, and Alex Rodriguez!)

There's been lots of online chatter regarding who J-Rod is and what he was in the past, and his account of its origins and its backstory is fascinating. The majority of the information comes from a person named Bill Uhouse, who claims that he worked with J-Rod. Uhouse claims he worked as an engineer in mechanical engineering in Area 51 and was partnered by J-Rod in the beginning. The mission was to build an air simulator that would help the human pilots to learn how to fly an alien craft.

According to Uhouse J-Rod was the acting technical advisor for the program that was classified as top secret. Also J-Rod, the alien, had been a government "non-terrestrial" agent. While it's not as unlikely it was a couple of years ago that an Scottish hacker by the name of Gary McKinnon appeared to prove the existence of such an odd position is actually present within the dark recesses of the U.S. government. McKinnon was slyly searching NASA's database of information on UFOs at the time he came across the shocking discovery.

While the name J-Rod has did not come to mind, McKinnon managed to seize classified documents that actually listed several "non-terrestrial" personnel assigned to secret military bases including Area 51. J-Rod could be one of the "non-terrestrial" officer. The 200-year-old alien was said to have been in the S4 area within Area 51, near the Papoose Mountain Range, ever from 1953.

The entity was initially introduced by military personnel of the U.S. military when his spacecraft crashed outside Kingman, Arizona. After locating the damaged craft they confronted its crew. Two were injured however, the remaining two were largely unaffected. J-Rod was just one of those creatures who weren't any worse off. Following some negotiations, the living ETs accepted to allow the human beings who had captured them to escort them into Area 51.

The remaining ETs started working with humans in the base. Uhouse states that as weird as it may be to have an alien serving as his superior one of the funniest things was that the alien was dressed with casual clothes of a human. Uhouse says that the 4-foot tall gray alien, with spindly legs and arms that had the standard facial characteristics of large eyes with black almonds, small nose, and a gap for a mouth, usually walked around dressed in a flannel blazer and a pair of Khaki pants. This would have been bizarre but fun certainly, especially taking something that the majority of people think of in their dreams and dressing him up in hilariously casual clothes!

Some who are familiar with the J-Rod story even claim that the 1980s sitcom Alf, whose plot revolved around a flannel-shirt-wearing alien who lived with a government scientist, was based on the story of Bill Uhouse's relationship with J-Rod at Area 51. It's a bit unbelievable that such sensitive materials would leaked to screenwriters from Hollywood However, there exist conspiracy theorists who claim that the government has used Hollywood as a tool for propaganda over the last several decades. They believe that television shows and films with extraterrestrial characters are made to gradually introduce the general public to believe that they do not have it all to ourselves.

It's likely that it was the way Uhouse remembers his encounters with J-Rod. Uhouse even sketched a famous photo of J-Rod that a former Air Force major who had seen the alien proved to be a striking resemblance.

Another reliable source originates from a leaker, who goes by the name "Kewper." He says that he was flown to S4 in the month of August 1958 to meet with J-Rod. Kewper was an expert in encryption and language that was charged with interpreting written and spoken languages of J-Rod's civilisation. Incredibly, it was one of the years cited in the latest CIA whistleblower who revealed at his funeral to having been on a tour of fact finding in Area 51 for Eisenhower--a tour that included an interview with aliens that was very as the one Kewper claimed to have been a part in.

Alongside the unidentified Kewper along with Kewper and Bill Uhouse, there is an additional whistleblower who is claiming contact with a mysterious alien being located in Area 51. The name of the whistleblower Dan Burisch. Dan Burisch and he is a microbiologist in the field. His work was at Area 51 was allegedly taking tissues from one of J-Rod's foreign partners (who will be referred to as J-Rod 2). Based on Burisch's account, J-Rod 2 was housed in the midst of S4 in Area 51. The living area was the "perfectly circular sphere" which was believed to be kept in quarantine-like conditions in order to safeguard J-Rod 2 from potentially harmful microorganisms.

The account of Burisch actually leaps forward when it comes to the timeline. For instance, the author claims that he got allowed to work at Area 51 in 1994. Although nearly forty years were gone by from the ETs were first introduced to the facility, the 200-year-old aliens who had a hankering for khaki pants were alive as they were ever. According Burisch, Burisch the fact that not only were J-Rods active and well and kicking, but that very flight simulator that they developed together with Bill Uhouse back in the 1960s and 1950s was operating.

Burisch says the simulator was displayed to him as a UFO simulator inside one of the hangars that were empty in S4. S4 facility. It comprised the "large piling with an gimbal that rotates." (For the rest who aren't so mechanically inclined, a "pylon" is essentially a huge horizontal platform. A the gimbal can be described as a pivoting support arm which can be attached to the craft, allowing for simulation of the rotation.) The alien discs were mounted on the apparatus to allow the flight simulation.

If we go back to the testimony by Bill Uhouse, it was likely in the year 1954 when Uhouse began work on the simulator alongside J-Rod. According to Uhouse the model which was tested in the simulator for discs did not contain motors or reactors. Instead, they had six energy capacitors that were in the exterior of the craft, which allowed them to generate small amounts of energy for the simulation tests.

The goal of all this was to put humans in for 30 minutes or so to familiarize them to the controls and what they could do with the vehicle in flight. In terms of the motors and reactors which would reside inside the actual flying versions of the ET aircraft, there's an additional eyewitness of Area 51 that we must mention: David Adair. Adair was said to have been an early prodigy and when he was a teenager, still in high school, he was already a pro in rocketry.

His incredibly sophisticated understanding of rocket engines that brought him the interest of officials in Area 51. According to Adair the administrators were so fascinated by his talents that on June 20th, 1971, they invited Adair to their most classified underground lab for a tour of one of the engines Area 51 scientists had been studying. The engine was in a way already familiar to Adair and he identified it as it was a "giant magnetic fusion containment device."

It was similar to ideas that he'd worked on previously but it was more complex than what he'd previously imagined. When he touched the engine and it appeared to react. The alloy of metal was warm and was able to change when he pressed it. Strangely yet, Adair began to get the feeling that the engine was similar to a warm blooded living and breathing thing; It was alive!

He stood on the his engine's top for a closer look. When he was looking around at different parts it became apparent that specific areas that seemed to be reacting to his presence by lighting up with occasional white and blue flashes. Adair proceeded towards the middle of the engine, and discovered several super-thin optical fibers "filled with a fluid" which were "cascading across the shell" of the motor or reactor alien to us.

He realised that these fiber optic cables could be nothing less than an artificial neural network. It was the equivalent of an artificially intelligent brain. As young as he was Adair was aware of the magnitude of the technology he was working with. Adair was shouting at the Area 51 guides below, "This device is much more than an engine! This is a power station! It must have come from the hull of a huge craft! Then where did it come from? ?"

His query was met with dismay and he thought about it loudly. "A vehicle like this would be manned by a team. What was the plan for these people?" And then, in a sign that he was unable to keep his sanity no longer, when standing on the machine from another planet, Adair blurted out, "This obviously isn't American or Soviet technology. It's from some sort of alien entity!"

While his guests were chatting on the ground, exchanging uneasy glances Adair kept on his rant "How old is this? Did you even dig it up? Are you sure it's millions of years old? Did you actually take the thing down?" The Area 51 crew was not satisfied but they were not satisfied. They dispatched the waiting army police to remove Adair from the pedestal on where the engine was parked.

Adair was sent home soon afterwards, and he has was never in contact with the people who lived at Area 51 for the rest of his life. He had seen enough this day to last an entire lifetime. Adair is of the opinion that engines such as those are put in UFOs in order to function as an advanced interface between crew and the vessel. Adair claims that it's this piece of "smart" tech that permits UFOs to perform the difficult breakneck speed maneuvers that have earned them fame throughout the years.

The aliens, he claims, are plugged into the engine's neural networks so that they are able to manage the ship by using their minds. The pilot becomes the vessel. This is why UFOs were observed performing amazing feats of evasive maneuvers for example, like the ability to dodge hot-spray missiles in the end of time as quickly as a child would avoid the rubber projectile during the game of dodgeball.

A famous clip taken from one NASA's spaceship missions, which conspiracy aficionados claim that a UFO is taking the kind of deflection. NASA's spaceship mission STS-48 was released on the 12th of September 1991. In orbit, the camera of the spacecraft captured what appeared to be mysterious objects floating in the air above Earth.

It is an instant flash that originates from someplace in the world And in the instant that the flash is observed it is observed that one object turns around and launches to the opposite direction with amazing speed. In a few seconds, a beam light can be seen shooting to space, from the point which the light was exploding beneath. Some conspiracy theorists believe that this is a UFO engaged in the same evasive movements that Adair stated, to protect itself from shooting towards the UFO from beneath.

Another witness of Area 51 tech who has presented similar assertions concerning this kind of technology for interactive piloting. The name of the witness was Philip Corso, and he was an World War Two veteran and an ex- Army Intelligence officer who successfully relocated more than 10,000 Jewish refugee from the dictatorship of Italian the dictator Benito Mussolini. Corso went on to provide in intelligence with the General Douglas MacArthur during the Korean War.

They are based on actual facts regarding Corso's personal life. However, Corso was a deceased in the year 1998, was later to claim that his profession took a radical left to the right shortly afterwards. Corso was taken to the office of the very first stage of the Central Intelligence Agency under Admiral Roscoe Hillenkoetter. Corso along with others was charged with acquiring all the information possible on the technology of aliens as well as debunking all sightings an ordinary person might have witnessed.

In his book The Day After Roswell, the author outlines in details the way alien artifacts were discovered in the aftermath of a disaster at Roswell and transported to secret locations like the outpost that was just beginning to emerge located in Nevada which would later become Area 51. Corso says that one of his personal items he observed was an alien head gear that was used as an interface direct between the pilot and craft. Similar to what David Adair intuited, this equipment was said to link both the pilot and the neural system that was in the ship, and synchronized his movements with the craft's ability to maneuver.

If this neural link-up is what people from Area 51 needed to get their aircraft to fly, it follows that the next process was to figure out how to alter it sufficiently to allow humans to use the system. Thus, a casting request sort of call was put out for the most brilliant minds who could be interested in this project. One of those genius minds was an aloof silent, reserved man who was named Bob Lazar.

Lazar says he was given an access pass to hangars in Area 51 as a research scientist during the fall of 1988. Lazar was escorted through the massive metal doors in the S4 building, which was located on the sides of Papoose Mountain Range to run tests of an unusual propellant technology. After Lazar was shown the machine he was going to develop, he became shocked to find that it looked similar to a flying UFO or flying saucer of a sci-fi film.

Lazar will later refer to this stylish saucer as"the "sport model" as a humorous reference to its slim design. It looked as if it was straight off the production line. Lazar smiled to himself while the thought occurred to him that he'd received a sneak peek into the most important hidden. It wasn't about aliens exploring the earth, but that those claimed alien vehicles were actually made up of top secret U.S. defense projects.

It wasn't until it was time to enter that the confidence in the issues he had to face was able to disappear completely. When he stepped into the vehicle, something "didn't make sense." He was struck by an frighteningly uneasy feeling that was hard to understand it, like that the air inside the vehicle was infused with a sort or strange force.

The second thing that was depressing was that the control room of the vessel was a bit small. Also, he noticed that the seats - which he believed those who piloted the vessel had sat on--were extremely small because they were supposed to accommodate people who were half, or perhaps one-third larger than an average adult. This was when Lazar began to realise the fact that it was not one of the top secrets U.S. plane that looked as if it was an alien spacecraft; it was actually an alien spaceship.

The realization struck Lazar with the force of a ton bricks. However, he refused to allow the shocking news to dampen his enthusiasm for the venture. Lazar immediately began working to reverse engineer the propulsion mechanism on the ship. Lazar states that the craft's propulsion system consisted of a series of gravity-amplifying devices that were located below the deck. The craft was able to defy the laws of physics and alter the gravity field at the will of its creators. One of Lazar's immediate duties was to determine the type of fuel that the craft could use to run.

According to Lazar He discovered that the craft was powered by what's known as "element 115" it was thought to be a bulky element, stored as gas or liquid inside small silver discs. It is the element that powered the craft's gravity amps. When Lazar first claimed this in 1989, he received a lot of dissented because elemental elements in the periodic table just reached the number 109.

However, when an innovation in the production of new elements in 2003, researchers began to create an element that was very similar to the one Lazar was describing in the past as "element 115" in the years prior. The element was only synthesized in tiny amounts, not even close to what Lazar said the saucer reactors he was working on ate, but the existence of this element was confirmed.

Even though some people criticize the new element is extremely unstable and deteriorates rapidly, Lazar says that this was actually the main reason. This material was not created in this universe, therefore it is not a surprise by the difficulty of replicate. Lazar insists that the element was made by ETs in a completely other planet with a completely unique chemical makeup.

Bob Lazar does predict, but he does predict that, after learning ways to improve their strategies Scientists should be able to modify the element so that it can be used in Earth too. There is a chance that -with just a some reverse engineering and possibly the help of Lazar's alien friends, the "sport model" may soon be in operation in the end.

Chapter 4: Which Base Is It?

Theorists of conspiracy have for a long time believed it is they believe that the United States has been secretly cooperating in secret with ETs to develop advanced technologies. But, it's not completely clear why these advanced aliens are coming to us and aid us humans with engineering and physics. How come our alien big brothers have to go through the effort to assist us with our math assignments? What's to gain?

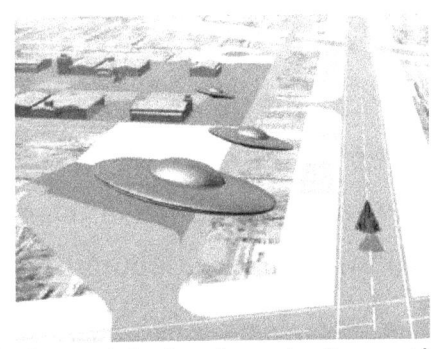

This chapter focuses on some possible theories as well as explanations which have been proposed as a means of explaining the nature of what these aliens are doing and who could be the ones in charge in Area 51. Like we said earlier in the report, it is believed that it was a section from the early CIA who first accumulated vast tracts of land to fund dark project aircrafts as well as clandestine investigations into the nebulous world of UFOs.

However, if we go deeper into UFO legends there is a claim that the CIA immediately preceded a more secretive organization known as"the "Majestic 12." It is believed that, shortly after Eisenhower's election in 1953, Eisenhower teamed up together with Nelson Rockefeller, then a part of the Council on Foreign Relations, and asked him to establish an unofficial study group to investigate the "alien issue."

The notorious "Capitol Hill UFO waves" where a variety of unknown craft swarmed into the skies right above the U.S. Capitol, had taken place just a year prior in 1952. The new President Eisenhower needed answers and wanted an elite team to gather these answers.

Rockefeller willingly put together the experts of the CIA and top scientists as well as top political operatives as well as military officers. The MJ-12 core consisted of experts such as the Dr. Vannevar Bush and Secretary of State James Forrestal who had already participated in the ET phenomenon under the presidency of Truman. Majestic 12 was said to have been established in Area 51 to oversee all experiments with ET technology.

There is a belief that this secretive organization is still at the helm of the Area 51. It's true that a significant amount of years have gone by since the creation of

Majestic 12 in 1953. And all of the founding members have passed away. What exactly is the composition of Majestic 12 now? According to conspiracy theorists this board of 12 members has changed when members pass away or quit. There is a claim that a prominent participant in the more recent years was the former the president George H. W. Bush.

The president Bush definitely was a qualified candidate for the ultra-secret intelligence agency as he served as head of CIA. Also, it is worth noting that Bush was known for telling reporters questions about his work at the CIA, "If I told you the things I was aware of you, I'd murder you." It was a joke to many. Others take the threat more seriously. They believe the members currently of Majestic 12, whoever they may be, will do the point of no return to protect their secret.

The report also claims that MJ-12 has since joined forces with other popular conspiracy theories like the Bilderbergers and the other councils of the known as the "New World Order." It was George H.W. Bush who was the one who famously declared in 1991 that the world was entering an "New Global Order" following the collapse of the Soviet Union. Some less conspiracy-minded observers are, naturally, pointing to the fact that, rather than talking about an invasion of the world, Bush was simply stating the obvious, We had come to the conclusion of Cold War with Russia and we were entering an era of change.

The conspiracy theorists also offer a counter argument (don't they often?). They think that this latest period of collaboration was prompted by an emerging ET threat, which prompted the expansion of MJ-12 internationally, and be able to attract former adversaries Russia to join forces. According to the theory, agreement between U.S. and aliens broke at some point in the 1970s or the early 1980s after the Americans realized that ETs were abducting and conducting experiments on a lot more people than was agreed upon, while simultaneously not meeting their commitments to provide operationally new technology. (So how much J-Rod!)

The tensions were said to have got to a boil in 1979, at a largely unnoticed location in Dulce, New Mexico. Because this book is on Area 51 we are not going to get into Dulce history too deep. The fact is that Dulce as well as Area 51 are thought to have a strong connection, as hardware and personnel flow across the New Mexico and Nevada bases through massive underground tunnels. One of the main differences is that ETs claim to have greater control of their Dulce base than at Area 51.

The control will be enforced more severely as you go deeper into the underground structure. Dulce Base is said to comprise seven levels. The three first floors don't seem particularly different in the way they are constructed and the top floor is just for security and maintenance, while the second floor houses shuttle trains and other forms of transportation as well as the third floor is home to human government office spaces. However, as the moment you descend beneath the third floor in Dulce the things begin becoming very odd.

Fourth floor believed to be used for studying psychic phenomena and programming of alien implant systems, while the fifth floor contains the human organs of deceased people, which are stored in amber vats that are a bizarre collection of liquid. In the deeper end, it's the sixth level that's considered to be the scariest. The floor is known as"the Nightmare Hall, this level is where some of the most sophisticated (and alarming) research is conducted. There, ET scientists run amuck by genetically altering human beings to get wings or tentacles. Spider legs, tentacles... you know what you're looking for, but with no explanation as to why.

The seventh and last floor of the ET-run base is believed to constitute a different type of storage facility. The floor is often referred to as"milk carton kids" floor "milk carton children" floor because it's said to contain thousands of unidentified and likely missing persons in a suspended state inside huge glass tubes. If all of this was real, it will show that the human race does not have any control over the actions of an alien being is attacking humans on this planet.

These things must be real to express such anger but the proof is sadly lacking. There are only anecdotal and secondhand accounts to draw on Dulce is more intangible as Area 51. These tales of ET-controlled facilities differ from stories of aliens being who were held prisoner and imprisoned in Area 51.

There is a clear conflict the existence of a handful of ETs being held captive by humankind in Area 51 and a large group of aliens are granted full control over the entire facility that is an auxiliary one in Dulce. Similar to many of the UFO mythology, the two stories appear to contradict each other as it's difficult to determine which thread of the story to trust.

Around 1988, at the same time as scientists like Paul Bennewitz were claiming that aliens held millions of people hostage in underground bases located in Dulce, New Mexico, an odd little film broadcast on the U.S. It was entitled "UFO cover up? Live!" and it was the first show to study the issue of aliens as well as UFOs that were active in prime time. Many are now convinced that this was an unsuccessful disclosure attempt from the federal government.

The programme featured whistleblowers, whose identities were hidden with their faces obscuring behind a shadow. They were referred to as the fake names of Falcon and Condor And the program was through these two men who gave the world its first glimpses into the events in Area 51. This show was the first that the word "Area 51" was used in a public manner and also marks the beginning of its use in the public vocabulary.

The film is fascinating by the details of the life of Area 51, especially its description of an alleged "alien captive"--the famous EBE 1, said to be held to authorities from the U.S. government. After that, it makes a strange direction as one informants explains EBE's love to eat strawberry ice cream.

There was a reason the spooky informant believed it important to note that the capturing ET was fond of eating strawberries Ice cream. Many believe that this absurd incident strategically placed at the final part of the program was deliberately used to spread disinformation in order that when people thought to think of Area 51, and aliens it would make them smile and then think, "Oh! What is that ridiculous nonsense about strawberries and aliens!"

Many felt that this phrase ruined a completely credible tale. Yet it is true that the real world is usually more believable than fiction. In that sense it is easy to ask the reason why people find it difficult to imagine that an ET that was forced to be a human for many years could not have some unique behaviors. Like eating strawberry Ice cream or sporting Khaki and flannel-colored shirts Perhaps?

There is evidence that suggests humans could not constitute the end all be all the all authority in Groom Lake. There is an abundance of evidence suggesting that there's an entirely separate part of the Groom Lake base, which is subordinate to those infamous "non-terrestrial" agents which hacker Gary McKinnon discovered in 2009. In addition, if we trace up to the works by Philip Corso and his experience dealing with the ET/U.S. government relationship, Corso claims that following

World War Two, the Eisenhower administration signed the process of negotiating a surrender.

And if the Americans have surrendered--albeit not unconditionally--that would lead you to believe that they are no longer the ones in charge of operations such as Area 51. The authority they once had was probably handed over by the ETs. There are other theories, such as an alien takeover or human abusers of aliens using strawberries There is an interesting third rail that reveals how the power structure of Area 51 is really all about.

It is believed that ETs collaborate with humans to deliberately increase the security of Earth in order to build a formidable allies against an unidentified "other danger" that grey aliens themselves are terrified of. Humans are considered to be the tough but sluggish barbarians, which aliens are attempting for armour to save them from themselves.

This programme of assistance to military forces to Earth is said to be known as Solar Warden. This program was used to develop a secret space defense system whereby mankind performs security work in space and the solar system. There you go lots of bogus powers for a base that is supposed to not exist.

They are the Everyday Workers of Area 51

With all the theories of conspiracy and all the wild talk surrounding Area 51, there are many people who participated in the activities of the base that did not lead to any fanciful claims. The following are the tales of people who worked in the ranks. They were able to get clearance at the base, and to work into a menial task however, they didn't have enough clearance to do other things.

This includes the kitchen staff, janitors and other maintenance staff that are essential to help make the facility work, including one like Area 51, which for the majority of their careers did not exist! In the case of an average Area 51 employee, a shift typically began with a flight to McCarran Airport located in Las Vegas, where they were able to board a plane belonging to the obscure "Janet Airlines" and then were transferred towards Area 51.

Janet Airlines is a series of passenger jets that are not marked by the Air Force, said to include 11 aircraft in all. The term "Janet" can be believed to be a slang term for "Joint Air Network to Provide Employee Transportation," but among the passengers who have traveled on Janet Airlines it's often used to mean "Just another non-existent Terminal." The joke helps to emphasize the bizarreness in Area

51, the infamous area that we were informed was not there.

While the majority of passengers on the Janet flight headed to Area 51 do not come to the airport with stories of aliens. All passengers require at least minimal security clearance to board the plane. Bob Lazar, who rode in Janet to work as a security guard at Area 51, even described the aircraft as divided into "classes" depending on those with higher levels of security.

People like him who had to work specifically on ET technology were basically detained as well as separated from other passengers within a restricted area. The segregation of those who were among the three traveling on the aircraft who knew the ET secret were separated from the other 250 passengers with no knowledge of additional top-secret events in the base.

According to some, this is the reason that although couple of whistleblowers, like Lazar are credited with amazing stories about UFOs and aliens. Many people have said that they had worked in Area 51 and never saw any evidence of this kind. The strict compartmentalization of data began at the Janet flight out of McCarron however it expands to all the activities at the base.

However, one aspect that could not be separated was the moment the moment that some of these daily workers discovered later that the radiation they'd received at the site caused the cancer they suffered from. Consider the case of Joe Bacco, who worked for a number of years in Area 51 as a low-level maintenance technician. Bacco as well as his crew's primary job was to maintain the condition of roads as well as other important infrastructure within the site.

Bacco was at the scene in Area 51 in 1970 when an underground nuclear test exploded and released waves of radiation upwards through the ground of the testing site. It also caused an effect similar to an earthquake. It caused huge cracks - as nearly three feet wide in some of the service roads that led to the facilities. The most damaging, however is the initial radiation. Radiation travelled on wind to a camp close by Area 12 where some 900 low-level workers and technicians were sheltered.

Some of them did not possess the necessary clearance for crossing over into Area 51 themselves, but the radiation emanating from the secret base did not discern boundaries or distinctions and they were all irradiated equally. Bacco and his team had the luck (or lucky) enough to be granted an B-level clearance that allowed them access to Area 51 for routine maintenance which is why he was among those that were brought in to perform emergency repairs on the deteriorated roads and damaged infrastructure that was just outside of the perimeter of the base.

Joe Bacco describes sizzling, "unbearably hot" asphalt that spewed out radiation and burned through their clothing. Sparks burst out from the pants he was wearing and his crew's ID badges quickly melted, and fused with their outfits. The majority of those that joined Bacco in this maintenance job to repair the runways and streets that comprised Area 51 are now deceased They are also eager to inform Bacco that he's lucky to be alive.

However, despite his efforts to make it through, it has not been easy. The fallout from the radiation must cause damage to Bacco's sweat glands because, after his radiation exposure during the 1970s, he's often soaked in sweat. It is impossible to take even a few steps on the floor without exchanging a shiver. The eyes of his are constantly swelling, which indicates damage to glandular tissue within the body. Yet, despite what everyone is saying, he's in good health. Many of his colleagues weren't so fortunate.

His supervisor at the job site, a guy known as Harley Roberts, died from cancer two years later after the incident occurred. However, Roberts did not die without fighting a battle, either legally or medically. In the process of launching one of the first attempts to make Area 51 accountable, he spent his last years devoted to an avalanche of lawsuits against the base, which legally did not exist.

Harley Roberts filed a lawsuit in which she claimed negligence on behalf of the mysterious base, seeking at minimum eight million dollars of damages. Naturally, there was there was no settlement however the case was ongoing long until Roberts died and was gone. While Area 51 whistleblowers in the UFO community would like to talk about the power of Area 51's reach, and the lengths they'll go in order for silence of witnesses the harassment by evil agents at the base was not the problem.

The biggest issue for the people who tried to bring Area 51 accountable for a poor working environment wasn't their fellow Men in Black, it was that they weren't able to prove they'd been employed at the base at all in the first place. A majority of the employees received their money in cash or by a different agency with no or official (or easily traceable) connections to the Base itself. Additionally, a lot of the employees had their information they could find about working in the public sector was erased when they left.

Without the ability to establish the work experience of their employees or the identity of their employer You can only imagine the difficulty it took for the injured employees to receive the compensation they deserve to ease their suffering. It's incredibly difficult to apply for workers' compensation as you're unable to prove your employment at all! Additionally, a lot of these dying patients also faced the possibility of being prosecuted for revealing their information. They still had to take an oath of security, and if they violated that oath, it could be punished with a maximum of 20 years in federal penitentiary.

In a state of inertia before the courtrooms, the victims ended up having to talk with an authority higher than them: President Bill Clinton. Clinton had become aware of the suit following the trial was concluded before the district court, the judge in charge, Philip Pro, requested for him to sign a document that any release of information in the Area 51 case, not even to help with the benefit of cancer patients would pose a threat directly for national security.

Bill Clinton did not hesitate to sign the directive which effectively ended the discussion and shutting the door to justice on behalf of the families of victims. This was all carried out in the name of national security. After leaving the presidency, Bill Clinton has in fact, renewed the directive (or in the case of as in the executive jargon, "Presidential Determination"). It turns out that the order was signed by him in 1995 needs been renewed each year.

So it is rather strange it is that Hillary and Bill Clintons (Bill Hillary and Bill Hillary) are both into the public record and stated they want to "get to the top of the mystery of Area 51"--when they're the ones directly accountable for a significant portion of the cover-up. Double-talk with relation to the base appears bizarre at best. The family members of the Area 51 workers don't take the situation very well.

One of the survivors who is named Stella Kasza, holds such hatred for the Clintons that she once told an reporter at The Washington Post that she would swear at the former president Clinton on his behalf for what he did to "her husband." It's something that almost everyone in Area 51 would seem agree with. However, Bill Clinton still contends that some matters relating to the death of her husband as well as the others who worked with his must be kept confidential.

The continuing decision grants Area 51 immunity from responsibility for a long time. Jonathan Turley, a distinguished faculty member of George Washington University's Environmental Law Advocacy Center, is among the handful of people that fight on behalf of the employees. Turley represented the husband of Stella's when he passed away and now is representing the rest of the workers and their families in relation to the what he believes as a scathing environmental violation within the workplace in Area 51.

Based on the experiences of these ex-Area 51 workers, the base has always been based on the "Mosaic Theory" which means that everything in the base is a an integral part of the larger picture. From the largest plane to the very last drops of fuel for jets each piece is crucial. The fear is that tiny amounts of chemical residues in machinery could be taken into a single piece by a hostile force and be used to figure out what type of experiment is taking place in the background.

That means all substances and chemicals that are not needed of all types must burn on site. Area 51's military authorities Area 51 is reportedly so committed to this, that employees have said they were asked to sort through piles of ash after the all equipment and chemicals had been burned to ensure that all of the materials were burned! The burning was reportedly carried out in the middle of Papoose Lake, just outside the notorious S4 installation.

One of the most tragic cases among Area 51 workers exposed to the deadly chemical was the case one of Robert Frost, who contracted a severe type of cirrhosis that affected the liver. The condition rapidly worsened and died in the year 1989. Frost was among those who had been instructed to sort through the piles of burning materials in order to confirm that it burned completely and no trace that was incriminating was left. The piles contained all the waste of the facility-- computers, documents medical equipment, documents, as well as leftover food items in the mess hall were systematically destroyed.

Given the drastic measures, a former Area 51 worker made the statement, "We were lucky they did not make us sort through our own waste since they forced us to sort through every other thing!" The most dangerous part of these burning and sifting practices was the chemical waste which employees were required to eliminate.

Though the government was unable to deny this claim while Frost still alive hazardous chemical compounds were found within the body of Frost during his autopsy. Massive amounts of dioxins as well as the trichloroethylene found in his body's tissues. All of these are highly poisonous substances that are not appropriate for use in the body of a human being. The fact to think that Frost had to be exposed these substances initially however, what's more alarming is that if just that the Area 51 authorities had come to the table, there could be a chance to spare his life. As you can see, up until Robert Frost died, no person knew what exactly the condition he suffered from. If the Area 51 maintained a log of the things their employees were often exposed to-- like many other facilities with high risk do, this would be of great advantage to doctors trying to cure Frost.

Chapter 5: What is the level of security in the area 51?

There is a claim it is Area 51 is the most safe building in the world. Earth. This is usually considered to be Gospel and nothing more can be said. It's not many people who want to try this fortress, which is supposed to be invulnerable. In this section we'll look at certain security aspects to a greater detail to provide an understanding of what's happening of the situation in Area 51.

The infamous "Camo Dudes" who watch the area around the base. There are countless motion detectors and cameras These are only some of the security measures which the courageous (or foolish) souls that have decided to enter the grounds of Area 51 have reported.

Before crossing the border of Area 51's official jurisdiction, There are a few remote sensors scattered all around the entire perimeter. The majority of them are magnetic and motion sensors which serve to monitor the movement of pedestrians and vehicles near the center. For a long time, Area 51 enthusiast and researcher Glen Campbell describes these sensors as "Easter eggs" because they're encased inside round plastic shells identical to the classic Easter sweets.

Beyond these perimeter Easter egg detectors, you'll see the very first signposts that state "photography is not permitted" and, perhaps more frighteningly, "use of deadly force permitted." If you pass by these warnings, you'll be potentially exposing yourself to battle with the Camo Dudes. They are the group who manages the outside security. Their name taken from their camouflaged attire. The heavily-armed soldiers take on trespassers swiftly and with aplomb.

The guards never reveal their identity. Their usual strategy is to shoot a weapon in the direction of a potential adversary and shout, "What the f--k are you doing? Take the f--k out this!" Although the ultimate the source of their employment cannot be determined with certainty however, for a long time it's been reported that they're employed by the security firm Wackenhut or, in the manner that is often referred to by critics, "Whack-a-Nut!"

The company is certainly getting some bad press for hiring loose cannons. It has couple of lawsuits to show this. But, it's highly regarded to deploy heavily-armed troops in its facilities. For example, at Area 51, the security guards have a high mobility- usually two men with armed guards driving a 4WD truck, and guard every square kilometer within the desert. If someone is able to cross the border into Area 51 these guards seem to have a sense of what's happening and rush immediately into the area of breach.

A couple of dirt bikers discovered this by accident after they attempted to cruise along the border towards Area 51 only to be rudely confronted by unhappy security officers who demanded they leave the premises. This hasn't ever been the norm. In 2010, a quite clever person tested the security of Area 51 on the spot by parking his vehicle at an appropriate location and going A-Teaming with the security team. He took his top-performing dirt bike/motorbike from the rear of the truck and down an incline, then headed directly for the main gate at Area 51.

Prior to the Camo Dudes figuring out the cause of their injuries they saw this man hurling his way through them in full velocity! The Camo Dudes were likely choking down donuts and coffee when they realised what had transpired! The person who trespassed caught the entire incident on video and you are able to view it on YouTube. In the footage of the incident, the security guards aren't there until after the man has returned his bike to his truck, and then is high-tailing them off of the scene!

This is certainly a severe security breach, the incident seems to be the only instance in its class. The more typical situation where an intruder is taken into custody by security personnel the suspect could be being held until police are able to arrive. If caught, trespassers will likely face a heavy fine (500 up to $1,000 dollars) or even a day in the jail for violating the law.

In addition to in addition to the Camo Dudes A different threat that one could come across when approaching the base are the helicopters in black. They are unmarked and black helicopters thought to belong to Area 51's traditional arsenal are known to come over people walking too near to the station. It is believed to be a deterrent technique; the pilots believe that the sudden roar of sound, wind and sand being hurled in the direction of the intruders' can convince them to turn back and head back home.

The recent increase in number of adventure seekers has resulted in numerous incidents similar to this around the borders of Area 51. It is not difficult to imagine that when the general populace was exposed to Area 51 in the 1980s by the fanciful stories of famous people like Bob Lazar, the security system of this hidden installation is certainly having plenty of work to do.

Instead of encroachments by inquisitive outsiders, the most significant risk to Area 51 security teams face may be the other security teams. Consider the Area 51 security report from 1982 that describes a circumstance which almost triggered a fight as well as the possible explosion of a nuclear weapon!

Richard Mingus, who was the security chief during that time, was working to transport a nuclear weapon into one of the testing locations at the time he was notified the fact that Area 51 was under attack. It was followed following by a response by the Department of Energy, with the voice of Mingus' radio saying, "Yes, we are being attacked."

The incident was confirmed by the sight of contact was observed with an unmanned helicopter that was hovering low and shooting at a guards group beneath. However, a few seconds after, the cause of the entire drama was evident: the hardworking security guards of Area 51 were told that they had a miscommunication. The helicopter actually fired blank shots during a typical routine exercise!

In the wake of this lapse in communications, Mingus would look back to that moment as the most terrifying experiences he's ever had in his experience in Area 51. Even though it only lasted only a short time however, the simple mishap got the attention of the FBI as well as officials at the White House as an occurrence that was of the most serious magnitude. In a short time, all knew that the secretiest base in the world Earth was in danger. However, as it turned out, there was not an danger from outside. All that was threatening the security of Area 51 on the day was misguided fear emanating from inside.

Area 51 and the War on Terror

In the months leading up to the 11th of September 2001, Area 51 was poised to alter the course of the course of history. In the past it was believed that a plan was being developed to murder an extremist Muslim leader dubbed Osama bin Osama bin. Before the 9/11 attacks, bin Laden had gained famous fame for being the mastermind behind the 1998 Kenya attack and attacks in 2000 on the USS Cole.

The time was when Area 51 was still perfecting the technique of making use of drones as a weapon for assassination.

They'd just built the Predator drone, and had loaded it with two Hellfire missiles bearing the bin Laden's name engraved on their side. To take off bin Laden, the CIA as well as other Area 51 authorities needed the consent from the president. In the initial months of his presidency, George W. Bush was hesitant to act.

It was more than just delayed action, but rather arose from worries about what sort of moral quandary approving random drone strikes could cause. At the time, there was not a precedent for this kind of action. This was a completely new area in a legal sense and the Bush administration was not looking to start the year in a way that exceeded its limits. Also, there was a huge worry about what's known as "collateral harm" that could result in wounded or killed civilians who were who were impacted by the explosion.

Within the area where bin Laden was holed up in, bin Laden had several family members that came and went throughout the day. One thing that Bush desired was to hear news reports regarding his decision to send an assassin robot to murder many females and kids. Therefore, the Bush administration decided to delay any action until they felt a little more sure regarding the outcome of a similar strike.

The CIA as a practice of providing a sharp analysis of the potential risks associated with every exercise they undertake, decided to take on this task and began to recreate the complete bin Laden compound. The replica was recreated all the way down to the last aspect into the deserts in Area 51 just to see what the impact of a drone strike using specially targeted Hellfire missiles might cause. The efforts were halted However, CIA Director

George Tenet decided it just was not worth it.

It's a given that Tenet was proven to be incorrect in a stunning fashion few months afterwards. In September 2001, the bin Laden-led Al-Qaeda terrorist group struck the twin towers of New York and the Pentagon out of DC which killed nearly 3000 victims. This must have been an affront to the analysts of the intelligence at Area 51 to realize that, with just a drone strike, they could have avoided the biggest tragedy in American the history of America.

A lot of top military officials had been averse to this idea until it was now evident that drones with weapons will be required within the newly-proclaimed "War against Terror." A few weeks later on September 28 the first drones had been operating surveillance missions in Afghanistan. The first drone attack during the war took place in November 2002 during which Yemeni terrorist Qaed Salim Sinan was incinerated with a strategically placed Hellfire missile launched by the Predator drone.

This attack demonstrated how it was possible for the U.S. military could specifically attack rogue actors, and then put them off the scene in good faith. The attack was followed shortly by another targeted murder one time of the highest-ranking official of Al-Qaeda known as Al-Harethi who was involved in planning the assault on the USS Cole just two years prior. The Predator drone tracked Al-Harethi over a distance of several miles before locating the best spot to hit the convoy. Within the secluded Yemen's Northwest Province, the command was issued to shoot the Hellfire missile directly at the car of Al-Harethi.

The explosion that followed proved it was clear that it was clear that the War on Terror was heating up. Unfortunately for CIA agents who had been working for hours to develop their roles in the war the assistant secretary of Defense, Paul Wolfowitz, was in danger of ripping it up.

In the news on a daily basis, Wolfowitz told CNN that the drone strike that occurred recently was an overwhelming victory. The reporter described the operation as an "very efficient strategic operation." However, this assertion was a negative one, creating the Yemeni government extremely uncomfortable. They were now forced except to reveal to the people of their country that they had been accepting their country to allow the U.S. to conduct lethal drone strikes inside their borders.

It triggered an immediate rebuke by the Yemeni government. They was likely to have supported the operation was the operation hidden. At this point then, drone strikes were placed in a new cloak of privacy. In the dark shadow of Area 51 anonymity that they began to make most impact on the War on Terror. In the years that followed, funding increased dramatically and within a short time, the next generation of drones were being taken off the production line.

It was a more modern variant of the Predator named Predator B. Predator B. It was far bigger than the previous model and had the capacity to hold more weapons like bombs guided by lasers. Similar to technological advancements in stealth during the 1980s and the early 1990s in the late 1980s and early 1990s, Area 51 gave its Air Force a tremendous edge. The Air Force now has the ability to be able to do some serious damage in any location and at any time using these multi-purpose drones.

It was clearly demonstrated in the event of March 29th in 2004, the day a drone operating in Iraq successfully snatched away four individuals who were on the verge of putting down the roadside bomb in order in order to take out U.S. troops. The drone was conducting surveillance close to Balad Air Base in northern Iraq and its cameras spotted those who were involved in this gruesome attack of subversion. The footage from the drone clearly shows terrorists putting up an explosive device on the roadway just outside the base. These devices were the most frequent cause of deaths for U.S. personnel for the recent years, and so the ability to capture criminals in the act and end their nefarious activities delighted the drone pilots.

This covert operation would last throughout the the Bush administration. They would ramp in intensity as the presidency of President Obama was in his Oval Office. Obama as well as the director of the CIA, Leon Panetta, began to depend on Area 51's drones to be an important instrument for the War on Terror. They depend on satellites to maintain an uninterrupted line of communication with their controlling units who are located at Area 51 (or whatever base they're operating from).

It is the Achilles heel of drone warfare. It's the weak spot in the drones' armor, which could become a target for those who have aggressive plans towards United States. United States. This vulnerability was shown in the case of Chinese in 2007, when they fired a missile that killed satellites to space and destroyed one of their satellites. It was an obvious demonstration of America United States that another nation could take away U.S. satellites and thereby interfere with their drones as well as their current War on Terror.

The fears caused by this resulted in a renewed desire to militarize space. The earlier plans for space war were abandoned during the 1960s after both the U.S. and the Soviet Union agreed to the Outer Space Treaty, which prohibited space-based weapons of war. In the 1960s, Americans as well as the Russians had been the sole people in a position to reach the space.

But, at the close two decades of 21st century we are witnessing numerous more actors pursuing the space. A few of them, particularly China, have plans to militarize whole areas of space. Since that the U.S. so dependent on satellite communication,

Area 51 has ramped the efforts to build protections from these threats.

Not that unfriendly nations are their only worry. They are also a major factor in the War on Terror rages on in the world, and if a terrorist group gained or received the technological capability to carry out their mission then you can be sure that that the U.S. satellite system would be the target of their ire. Area 51 is working harder than ever before to develop security measures to counter multiple threats - if needs be, and all the way into the void of space.

Chapter 6: The beginnings of Disclosure or Misinformation?

In the past decade the 1980s, an incessant flow of bizarre information has been intentionally leaked from the area 51. The reason behind this leak is still unclear. Many think that the government is seeking to slowly ease us into and get us to feel more comfortable (if this is even feasible) with the strange happenings in Area 51.

Other people, however, hold different theories. They think that the government has been using reports of aliens and UFOs as a cover-up for the government's own secret plans. They believe that the eerie smokescreens coming from Area 51's chimney are another example of similar to the ones that were previously seen. According to them, the sudden surge in talk concerning the mysterious connection between Area 51 and aliens during the latter half of 1980 was purposely designed to draw attention away from the stealth plane program.

The promises were believed to have started by introducing the AMOCO alien. It was an incredibly innocent advert that was published in Aviation Week and Space Technology. The advertisement showed a real, realistic image of an alien being raising its hand in either a gesture of affection or asking the question. It was accompanied with the tagline "Technology to the point that it could assist you in answering some major problems."

The magazine is famous for facilitating Area51's leaks, this shocking image of an ET prominently featured on page 51 seemed to many to be a bit strange. Are the creators behind this ad trying to address some of the most important questions regarding Area 51's connection with aliens through the display of the ad featuring an alien on the 51st page in the publication?

According to certain sources, the government has been publishing slowly but steadily of data regarding UFOs and aliens for a long time. According to them, this could possibly be a genuine photo of an alien placed in a typical publication advertising. The real story could come to the public in a way, however, without having any consequences because the people behind it can be able to always discredit the real story that lies behind it. Should they be later questioned the person behind it could claim that it was just the result of a joke or an adorable commercial.

The famous "UFO cover up? Live!" broadcast in 1988 is believed to be an instance of this type of humorous announcement. The real information was then mixed with funny disinformation (like aliens consuming strawberry Ice cream). Then, the officially-approved leaks are believed to have led the creation of a show named Cosmic Journey.

The idea was an interactive tour which the government could finally reveal some of the information regarding Area 51 and UFOs. According to research, the idea was scrapped at the final minute due to the discovered that the general public was not ready to accept the information. If this is the case then it's likely that there's a degree of tension between the many groups within the industrial complex (as Eisenhower called it).

There is a possibility that some are close to disclosing more information however, they had to pull away just in case due to fears about national security. It appears that there are two primary forces operating at the base, those who support transparency and those who are refusing to give it up.

What if there were another force blocking disclosure in every way? What if that group was actively informing the elected representatives of our country?

The 2016 presidential election in 2016, the unlucky campaigner Hillary Clinton promised to get into the facts about Area 51 (her husband's presidential conceal-up orders regardless). The seemingly innocuous announcement of this unusual undertaking shocked many who read it as completely absurd. The question is how Hillary could have actually followed the plan is now a non-issue issue since she did not be able to win the presidential election.

The woman lost, naturally against an individual who was positioned as a wrecking ball in opposition to the accepted procedure. Is this one-man wrecking squad able to be the first to break through the barriers of secrecy surrounding Area 51? It is possible that brazen billionaire President Donald Trump would--perhaps on some impulse of a knee-jerk, launch an investigation into Dreamland?

Trump has indeed established himself as a target easy for the establishment to choose. Take a look at his controversial assertion that the president Obama came from Kenya as well as his ties to the conspiracy-crazed Birther Movement. Obama himself was famously mocked by his fellow president Donald during his White House Correspondents' Dinner in a speech that urged Trump to "get back to the matters which really matter, like was it a hoax to fake the moon landing? And what actually transpired during the events at Roswell?"

You could certainly include Area 51 to that jokingly mentioned collection of conspiratorial theories. The Trump administration has been largely silent on the subject. We have only heard some odd remarks that Trump made during his inauguration. Trump said at his inauguration: "We stand at the beginning of the new millennium and are prepared to discover the secrets of space, and to liberate our Earth from the ravages of sickness, and make use of the energy, industries and innovations of the next century. The new sense of pride in our nation will inspire us raise our heads and heal our divides."

A lot of people were shocked by the announcement of the new president, given that there was no indication of desire to pursue such a subject prior to this. If you look at it in the context of the whole talk about harnessing the "energies of tomorrow," industries, and the technologies of the future" seems like it's an advert to promote Area 51 itself. It could be a further story of denial and disinformation all wrapped up in one giant assortment of conspiracy theories.

A second aircraft is believed to be located

in Area 51

Whatever else, Dreamland has a long and fascinating history of being the location where some of the world's most sophisticated aircrafts are constructed. We are aware it was the place where U-2 spy aircraft as well as the SR-71 Blackbird, the Stealth Fighter and Predator drone Predator drone were developed at Area

51. The information is now classified, open to the public. However, at one point it was classified, even if one had to make a report of seeing these aircraft in the sky the existence of them could have been ruled out.

Now that these once classified craft are out to the world and available for inspection, you begin to think about what the engineers working at Area 51 are working on currently. This isn't like they've removed their equipment and shut down after they perfected the Predator. Common intuition tells us it's likely that Area 51 must be playing hosts to all kinds of high-tech craft.

In the last thirty years, Dreamland has been able to design and build aircraft that go beyond the wildest expectations. In this article, we'll look at every aircraft being developed and some of the latest designs that have been made available to the general public. These are the most famous names mentioned in the past.

The Aurora

The Aurora is most likely to be one of the most praised among all the objects believed to be hidden in Area 51. It is interesting to note that it was first brought to the public's attention because of a typographical error. In the event of some mistake that led to the project's black color, Aurora was included as an item within the annually updated Fiscal Procurement Program document from February 1985.

In the middle of the day there was a thing was called Aurora was classified under the classification in "Other aircraft" and is expected to get up to 2 billion dollars of funding! This is a pretty significant price for a plane that was never intended to exist. However, it is evidently worth it all.

This aircraft is said capable of reaching the speed of Mach 6 speed, which would suggest it can easily travel up to 4,500 miles at an hour.

When the Aurora was believed to have been observed by engineer for oil rigs Chris Gibson in 1989, the Aurora was operating at a more sluggish rate. It was being escorted by two F-111 aircraft, it seemed to be trying to get together to refuel using the Boeing KC-135 Stratotanker. (The Stratotanker is a massive transporter of fuel that is used by the military to refill aircrafts during mid-flight.)

Gibson had grown accustomed to witnessing this fluttering gasoline station and recognized exactly what it was. He was also familiar with the F-111s. However, the mysterious triangular aircraft trying to connect with the Stratotanker was completely new for

Gibson. The plane was unlike anything previously seen, and for someone who was a self-proclaimed aviation professional, that was a huge statement. The aircraft was huge and had no "gaps" or "wings"--just an ideal isosceles triangle.

Gibson wrote the bizarre aircraft to his memory when it was possible, he sketched a simple picture of the plane. This sketch was featured alongside recent speculation and rumors regarding Aurora within the November 1992 issue of the aviation/military periodical Jane's Defense. This is where the first time it was claimed that Aurora was capable of achieving some kind of suborbital flight. It was also claimed that the Aurora would be able to reach anywhere within three hours. The Aurora craft was also believed to have Aurora was powered by Aurora craft was powered by the special liquid methane.

The sightings on the ground of the aircraft would be forthcoming over the next few years But perhaps most importantly, there have been numerous incidents of pilots from commercial airlines traveling across -- and sometimes almost colliding with triangular aircraft that appear to correspond with Gibson's descriptions of the Aurora very perfectly. Which is the final word about this infamous high-flyer that came from Area 51? It's up to us to see.

TR-3A Black Manta TR-3A Black Manta

The mysterious craft is thought to be a subsonic stealth plane like the Aurora however it is the more delta-like flying wings. Many sightings have been recorded of the craft, mostly in the southern part of California as well as Nevada. The craft was also believed to have made an appearance during the Gulf War, where some say they saw the Black Manta helping F-117 Stealth

Fighters with the laser-guided sights it has to send targeting data to the aircraft. It is believed that the Blank Manta is commonly believed to be an improved variant that of B-2 Stealth Bomber.

Chapter 7: Tacit Blue

The aircraft that has been rumored for years is actually discovered to be real and has been proven. It has the appearance of the whale and is now the unpopular name of Shamu. Don't let the lighthearted name fool you, this plane was meant to be a the business. The plane was intended to function as an air platform that was hidden behind the lines of enemy troops, shielded from radars, so that crew could relay intelligence into friendly territory, then aim the use of missiles, bombs and other weapons at targets immediately. Tacit Blue was to be the command center that could multitask during World War Three, but when it became apparent war was coming to an end, Cold War was coming to its end, Tacit Blue was decommissioned. The mysterious craft is currently in an open-air museum located in Ohio.

The primary reason for the plane's peculiar box-like (or like some might say whale-like) appearance is to deflect radar. It was decided that a small-flying surveillance aircraft would require an entirely different style than those of "hopeless diamond" type stealth fighters or bombers. The radar deflection specifically focused on head-on collision with radar. However, a aircraft like Tacit Blue, designed to constantly be circling a battlefield collecting intelligence and gather intelligence, required the same boxy appearance to block radars from every side. It's true that the design may work more to "redistribute" radar, rather than be able to deflect it. However, however it performed to deflect radar, it left Tacit Blue completely unrecognizable to adversaries' air defenses beneath.

It was discovered that the greatest challenge to the development of Tacit Blue was to get it in the air at all. The unusual shape, though useful for long-term evasion of radar, rendered the aircraft only a tiny bit not aerodynamic! Tacit Blue was actually one among the less-known mysteries that was part of Area 51, but now it's an actual piece of historical significance.

Bird of Prey

The secret weapon was revealed just in time for the upcoming war in Afghanistan. A year ago it, thousands of Americans were brutally killed by militants from Afghanistan, a war-ravaged country. this time, this Bird of Prey was doing its best to bring vengeance against those responsible for the murder of thousands of innocent civilians.

It's a funny coincidence that the plane that was tasked with revenge for the loss of lives on 9/11 first took off on the 11th of

September in 1996. The plane is named in a humorous way after Star Trek's Bird of Prey spacecraft from Star Trek, it is claimed to be flying at 300 miles per hour and maintain stealth capabilities even during the daytime.

It's not comparable to similar Area 51 creations that reach more than 22,000 miles per hour however, it is clear that the Bird of Prey was developed to be a versatile machine, not for its speed. It serves as a trusted multi-tasking tool during the War on Terror quite well.

In terms of what Area 51 is currently working on? That's anyone's guess!

Our Day in the Sun

Space 51 has to be without no doubt one of the most strange and most enigmatic places around the globe. In the middle of nowhere, but equipped to the brim and kept in complete secrecy the base was believed to be in a state of non-existence. The refusal to acknowledge the existence of a whole military facility that sets Area 51 apart from the beginning.

There are numerous bases in the United States that oversee classified materials and projects, however these bases aren't classified as classified. Area 51 is, however is said to extend hundreds of miles in size and has the longest runway in the nation but until recently, the existence of Area 51 was debunked.

What kind of activity is significant enough to warrant a massive base of activity needed to be classified and buried and hidden from American general public? This is the query that has been asked by people for a long time, and the inability to answer it is what has led to the mystique and imaginative theories were developed with regard to the area that is known as Area 51.

It is true that things aren't considered to be fanciful or fantasy until they're proven to be real. Stealth technology stands as a testimony of this. Before the introduction of the very first Stealth Fighter, the idea of a plane capable of making it invisible to radar was thought to be an idea for science fiction.

As long as they weren't willing to update the rest of us about the specifics Area 51's folks Area 51 were quite happy to tell us that the sighting of an aircraft was no more than the imagination of a child. As it was revealed during the Gulf War revealed, such objects do exist.

Although the stories of alleged events in Dreamland that are described in this book might appear to be, they may just be as amazing in the time that the people who oversee Area 51 want them to be. Perhaps, just maybe, one day Area 51 will have a vast array of new surprises that are waiting to be discovered by all of us.

We're hoping to all get a day in the sun in Area 51! Thanks for taking the time to read!

Thank you for buying and reading the book Area 51"What They Don't Like to Say! I hope you enjoyed it. Since I am a self-published author I am always interested in hearing what my readers think of my book. If you've got time to review my book, you can do so on Amazon click here.

Additional Reading and Reference

We're at the conclusion of this book, I'd suggest some references and reading resources that made the project possible. If you'd like discover more information concerning Area 51, I suggest to familiarize yourself with the great sources listed below.

Dreamland. Phil Patton

In this novel the journalist and investigative reporter Phil Patton goes on a excursion to see the sights of Area 51. Although he's naturally, unable to visit the actual base however, he tries his best to look around the outside and explore the various local spots of interest in the region. While doing so encountering an array of people who are insiders or theorists. He is a master at how he combines their diverse views into one cohesive treatise about the basis that was never meant to exist!

Zone 51: Black Jets. Bill Yenne

The book stays clear of the conspiracy theories and theories and focuses on real, verified truths in regards to Area 51. The story is a simple and straightforward description of the past of the construction of aircraft in the area starting with to the U-2 spy plane, to the Stealth Bomber and beyond. The book offers a comprehensive overview of the development of technology within Area 51.

The Revelations: Alien Contact and Human Deception. Jean-Jacques Valleee

Jacques Vallee is a true legend in the world of Ufology and his thoughts regarding Area 51 are rather eye-opening. The author delves into the many details of the topic, as well as his unique research and conclusion are not to be overlooked.

A day After Roswell. Philip Corso

The book's primary focus is about Roswell and his experiences, the perspectives of the former intelligence officer who claimed to have access to some documents that, according to UFO mythology--would be eventually sent towards Area 51 make for a interesting reading. The book tells another story told by eyewitnesses that is to be wildly absurd but is it is also incredibly impossible to overlook.

Philip Corso was at the close of his existence when he revealed his part in the battle against alien technology And he went on to the grave swearing up and down that everything claimed to be the truth. If the man wasn't mentally ill, it's unlikely that he'd tell many lies on the grave. This book offers a quantity of details that seem to be similar to a lot of others that have come out of Area 51.

The Dulce Book. Branton

It is possibly one of the more absurd works ever published in the realm of UFOlogy. It is nevertheless useful, as Dulce is another notorious basis of UFO legends. It is possible that none of this is real, however the curious story of the supposed Dulce base provides an insight into the truth regarding Area 51.

The Close Encounters in Capitol Hill. Robert M. Stanley

The novel is distinctive due to its broad array of stories, all linked in a way to Washington, D.C. It is however the chapter dealing in Area 51 that is the most intriguing. It tells the story of the famous engineer David Adair and his experience dealing with the "alien engine" which appears to have originated from the Disney film Flight of the Navigator.

This film follows the story of a boy in his early teens who comes to contact with an alien spaceship, and then connects to the spacecraft's nerve system in order to pilot it. David Adair said he experienced exactly the same experience in his engine from another world, according to him, it was responding immediately to his thoughts and feelings. Actually, his account closely resembles Flight of the Navigator so many times that it's easy to think that the deceased engineer (he died in 2009) invented his entire tale by taking from the film.

However, as frequently is the situation with UFO legends, it's difficult to determine what came first: the egg or chicken? Did Adair have a look at a film that was the catalyst for him to develop the story of a UFO, or could someone else have witnessed a UFO enticed to create a screenplay about the subject?

Theorists of conspiracy theories, after all claim that the majority of science-fiction films that came out in the 1970s and 1980s were influenced by leaks from the government of true incidents. On the other hand this book contains intriguing rumours of insider knowledge regarding what might be hidden inside the confines of Area 51.

Chapter 8: A New Beginning

It is not clear how the initial events of the incident ought to be documented in the proper manner. There are reports that indicate that in the evening on July 1st 1947, radar detected objects that were flying more quickly than any aircraft that was known to mankind could ever fly in their radars that were located in Roswell, Alamogordo, and White Sands. In the early morning of the following day people began making calls to the Roswell police, claiming that they've seen odd objects flying in the skies. Radar continues to record bizarre tiny blimps of radar that are which planes can't do.

On the evening of July 4th an intense thunderstorm swathes the Roswell region. While Steve Arnold is watching the radar, he sees an object that has been making bizarre hairpin turn and seems to be traveling at around 3000 miles per hour.

After which, it disappears off the radar. Then telephones in the local sheriff's department and at the local police department are ringing as people have reported hearing a loud, crashing sound.

In the year World War II had ended only two years prior the end of World War II, the Colonel William Blanchard goes on high alert, thinking that an adversaries are attacking his headquarters. He quickly dispatches a group which rushes towards the location of the accident. One of them who arrives at the scene as per the account are Steve Arnold who says he saw a disc with a crescent shape that was almost entirely intact. Arnold was a professional who has been working for his entire career in various airplanes, states that he's astonished since he is aware that an aircraft could have smashed into million pieces. However, this one was nearly completely in good condition.

Arnold is also reported to have observes a number of gray bodies close to the aircraft and he sees an alien that is still alive. The soldiers are said to have fired at the alien and kill the creature on the spot. Because the soldiers are concerned the possibility of a fire bursting so they ask for help from firefighters from the Roswell Fire Department as well as fireman Steve Dwyer, who has reported gazing in the direction of the alien that transmits messages to let it know that it's dying.

The sun's rising light begins to rise above the horizon, many people living nearby report that they are aware of the noise and decide to go toward the scene. One of the people who arrive at the spot includes The Dr. W. Curry Holden, archeology professor traveling together with students from Texas Tech University, James Ragsdale and Trudy Truelove, who were camping near the hills. Sergeant Thomas

Gonzalez and Major Edwin Easley who written affidavits stating that they were assigned to protect the vessel, Steve MacKenzie who claims that he was accompanied by a group of soldiers from Washington D.C. to the location, as well as mortician Glenn Dennis who claims that the mortician received phone calls asking for how to get three small coffins. Each of them was or were leaders within their respective communities. How come they collaborated in telling a story that is difficult to be believed?

In addition, Dennis says that he needed to get to the hospital for other reasons on the same evening the incident was initially announced. Dennis claims that when his way to the hospital, there were two ambulances that had their doors opened at the back. The man claims that hanging out of the doors of the ambulance were a number of fragments of debris. What caught his eye were fragments of which appeared to be metallic material with particular decorations. The man says after studying them for just a couple of seconds after which he ventured into the hospital and met a nurse knew. When he stopped and said thank you to the nurse He claims to have been rudely confronted by two police officers. They escorted Dennis out of the premises.

On the next morning, Dennis claims that the next day he had lunch with the nurse. The nurse was extremely concerned over what she saw in the hospital that morning. The nurse says that she was asked by two physicians to conduct autopsies on two corpses which were not humans. Being a fervent Christian She was worried that she thought about taking a break from her work.

There are many who wonder who the nurse was, and then try to undermine the credibility of Dennis as he did not reveal her identity. Do you think he felt a need to shield the nurse? Many believe that the people who were present on that day were warned to stay quiet. If this is the case and it was the case, Dennis might be feeling a need for her to come out independently. To date, she's declined to take that step.

It is up to you to choose whom you trust on your own, but a large portion of the evidence appears to favor one view. However, the opposing faction seems to debate. There is no definitive evidence of what transpired during the day in the high plains. day.

You Still Do Not Like the Beginning

There are reports that offer a distinct version of what transpired. They say that the moment that Brazel was visiting the sheriff on Monday morning, he brought pieces of debris along to take with him. The sheriff then called his Air Force officials who assigned the officers to examine the matter Brazel noticed.

The reports state that the items that were handed over to Wilcox was immediately taken and seized by The Air Force who had already reached Major General Clements McMullen, Commander of the Strategic Air Command his commander. Based on these accounts, McMullen has requested a container containing the contents to be put on an airplane, and transported directly to the Fort Worth Army Air Field at which the plane is greeted by the colonel Thomas DuBose. Based on these reports the box will be tied to DuBose's hand. The Colonel then is then able to jump on a B-26 aircraft as well as the box. Then, Colonel DuBose are taken straight into Washington D.C.

According to these reports, there's more trash than Brazel admits to having seen. According to these reports, the waste that was that was taken to Wilcox's office weighed in at one station wagon, and after the two men had finished cleaning the debris field, they had gathered enough debris enough to fill two station wagons.

Based on these accounts, Marcel stops at his residence on his way back and is able to show some objects to his wife as well as his son. Marcel's son, who was just eight when he was discovered, eventually became secretary of state of Montana. He states that he can clearly recall the tinfoil he found at the location, due to the fact that it was a distinctive. The material is described by him as extremely thin similar to the thickness of tinfoil in a packet of cigarettes, yet it was extremely difficult to stretch.

Marcel was a staunch supporter of the federal government, and remained silent about what transpired that night until the year 1972. In 1972, he recorded a tape interview on what he observed in the field on that particular day. The material he saw was not an aircraft missile or a weather balloon. The material is described by him as "other in the world." He claims that it will not burn, it was extremely thin and did never bend. He said that it was extremely thin and would not bend. Marcel went to his final resting place and declared that it was a disc of flying found in the grassland. Marcel's perspective on this matter is crucial as he was one leading leaders in the sole atomic bomb organization that existed in the entire world.

You must pause and think about what could be the cause of so many disparity in the events of people who led or who became leaders within their respective communities. Could it be that Brazel was paid to stay from speaking out or the family he was with could be hurt if he did speak up? In other accounts those who witnessed UFOs who were community leaders, report that they were harassed by black men that threatened their lives. Was the same thing happening to Brazel?

Chapter 9: Initial News Reports

On July 7, Lydia Sleepy was employed as a teletype operator for the local station for news. In the early morning, she said she was notified of a call from her boss, as well as the her local ABC station director John McBoyle telling her to be in the office as soon as possible. The woman claims she was in the process of transmitting the story that John McBoyle knew about the incident and a message popped up on her telepath system, saying ""This will be the FBI so you should stop broadcasting." The story did spread rapidly there were headlines across all over the world announcing that the military had announced the existence of the flying disc in an ranch in New Mexico. The reports were made by first lieutenant Walter Haut who claims that they are acting under instructions from the commander of the base, Colonel Blanchard.

The story that was published within the Roswell newspaper's local Roswell newspaper on the following day, under the headline "RAAF Capture Flying Saucer on Ranch in the Roswell Region" stated,

The office for intelligence that is part of 509th Bombardment unit located at Roswell Army Air Field has announced in the afternoon that the area has come with flying saucers.

According to the information provided by the department under the authority of Major. J. A. Marcel, intelligence officer, the disc was discovered from a property within the Roswell area, following an unidentified rancher had informed Sheriff Geo. Wilcox and here that he'd discovered the device at his property.

Major Marcel along with a member of his division visited the ranch and recovered the disc, the report said.

Once the officer in charge of intelligence was able to inspect the device, it was taken to the more senior headquarters.

The CIA said that there were no specifics about the saucer's design or design were revealed.

Mr. and Mrs. Dan Wilmot apparently were the only people living in Roswell who saw the what they believed was an erupting disk.

The couple was sitting on their patio at 100 South Penn. Last Wednesday night, it was around 10:00 p.m. when a massive bright object glowed into the sky towards the southeast. It was moving towards the northwesterly with a rapid rate of velocity.

Wilmot was able to call Mrs. Wilmot's attention and they both went down to the yard to look. There was just under (sic) one minute maybe 40 to 50 minutes, Wilmot estimated.

Wilmot stated that it seemed to him that it was around 1500 feet in height and was going quickly. Wilmot estimated that it was somewhere between 400 and 500 miles per hour.

It appeared to be similar to two saucers that were inverted, facing from mouth to mouth or as two antique washbowls that were arranged, like a pair. The whole thing glowed like light was shining out from within, however this was not the case however it was not the way it would if lighting source were just beneath.

From the position he was in, Wilmot claimed that the thing appeared to be around 5 feet tall taking into account how far it was away from town, he calculated that the object must have been about 15 or 20 feet in size however this was only an estimate.

Wilmot claimed that he was unable to hear anything, however the Mrs. Wilmot said she heard the sound of a swishing during a short period of time.

The object appeared from the southeast before disappearing above the trees in the vicinity around Six Mile Hill.

Wilmot the man who is among the most admired and trustworthy citizens of the town was hesitant to reveal the details of his experience in the hope that someone could come along and share their experience of seeing the thing, and then made the decision to be the first to tell of the experience. The news that the RAAF had possession of one was made just a few minutes after Wilmot decided to make public the specifics of the incident he witnessed.

A few years later, the writer in Aliens Everything You Want to Know says he conducted an interview with Walter Haut. Walter Haut who substantiated this account. Walter. Haut passed away in 2005.

Although small towns like Roswell have a reputation for spreading reports of UFOs, one has to wonder whether a lot of people could be right. For instance, in the past when there was stigma associated with the belief that UFOs were real. This stigma persists to this day as only one per three people believe that UFOs exist. Naturally, it is important to ask what transpired during the time of that field.

Is it a weather Balloon?

In the morning However, by the next morning it was discovered that by the next morning, however, Air Force had changed their claim that their original report was false and claimed that the military found an air balloon. The Air Force was now asserting that it was the weather balloon developed under Project Mogul. It is clear that the project was Project Mogul, a top classified weather balloon that contained microphones. But, you have to consider asking different officials from the military present on the ground what they could have done to identify a weather balloon however it may have been made a bit differently from the ones seen prior to. Though weather balloons have gone out of fashion, they were quite common back at the time, with several sites sending frequently which included close to Alamogordo, White Sands, and Roswell. Thus, lots of individuals, not even associated with the military might have seen an air balloon.

On the 8th of July 1947, around 3 pm in the afternoon Brigadier General Roger Ramey announced to the public that the flyer was to be sent into Wright Air Force

Base in Ohio. But, in less than two hours the general Clements McMullen called Colonel DuBose and asked him to deliver part of the wreckage in the direction of Washington D.C. and the remaining for Wright Air Force Base. It was also reported that he instructed DuBose to create an excuse that the debris was a weather balloon in order to keep journalists out of their backs. When he died in 1991, DuBose stated that he received a phone message by General Clements McMullen in Andrews Army Air Field declaring that General Ramey was in charge of a cover-up in order to remove the media from the military's backs.

The initial reports at the scene claim that DuBose was tasked with transporting debris towards Fort Worth, Major Jesse Marcel claims that he was responsible for the transport. The debris occupied half of the B-29. The biggest weather balloon of that time wouldn't come close to this size.

In the early hours of 5:15, Irving Newton, a young weatherman, was summoned to go to Ramey's office. The officer, who was young, was hesitant to go from his desk however, he followed the orders. The reason Newton was hesitant was because the weather desk is never to remain unmanned. However, Ramsey insisted and the official was forced to comply with his instructions.

Reporters were not convinced and, at around 8 pm Ramey was interviewed by the media for a second time. He claimed that he'd committed a mistake, and the story was a simple weather balloon. After that, the media removed the story, and they agreed to the revised story.

Many people are wondering what the reason why the government worked to conceal the fact that UFOs crashed into the New Mexico pasture.

Did it look like a balloon, or a floating disc? You'll have to come an informed decision for yourself. There are many aspects you should consider prior to making a ultimate choice. At first, the trained personnel couldn't identify a meteorological balloon, regardless of their popularity in the vicinity. A lot of people with a strong name were eventually able to come forward to report seeing an air-borne disc. A mortician who is young in Roswell claims to have been contacted concerning the availability of three caskets for children. If you believe Marcel carried the remains into Fort Worth, then he states that the debris is too large to qualify as a balloon. Also, one must consider the reason Ramey was not in a rush to rectify the situation.

Most viewers have seen the iconic photograph of an army officer in his youth standing with the various elements of the balloon. This photo was not released in the 20 years that followed the incident in the year Look Magazine did a feature report about UFOs. There is a need to consider what it was doing all the period.

Also, one must stop to consider the victims who were reported to be transported to the scene of the accident. There are various reports that show many people were at the scene. The most often mentioned present was the members from the General Advisory Committee of the Atomic Energy Commission which included J. Robert Oppenheimer often credited as the father of the Atomic Bomb as well as the later leader of the influential General Advisory Committee. Many members of Operation Paperclip were also seen. They were Germany specialists in rocketry that came in this area of the United States during and immediately after World War II. They included Wernher von Braun, who was the main person responsible for the German missile program as well as the pioneer of space medicine Doctor Hubertus Strughold. The other person to be reported included Theodore von Karman who is an Jewish Hungarian aerodynamicist.

In addition to the story about the weather balloon that was not logical to the vast majority of people who were on the scene and also the military not divulging this information until next day, this story is not without a problem. Albert Crary who was responsible for weather balloons within the area, wrote in his journal that they were unable to fly balloons during the day due to the cloudy weather.

In the past, individuals have attempted to prove that the corpses that witnesses claimed to have seen in the area were made of wooden test Dummies. This theory could be a big issue. It is not clear if the use of test dummies in the next six years.

Furthermore, one should think over a second aspect. Most people who make errors in identifying UFOs as an actual weather balloon will be severely punished in the army. The minimum is that they're not promoted and in most cases, the military forces are forced to retire, or the worst. However, that was not the situation for Colonel Blanchard. He was promoted quickly and within a short period of time, he was promoted to Vice Chief of Staff for the United States Air Force. We have to wonder if the military officer was exceptionally gifted that he decided to go in opposition to the norms of military or did the most powerful individuals on earth must buy his silence.

It is obvious what the purpose of all these specialists being needed on the scene in case the weather balloon fell. Weather balloons were quite common during the past.

Thirty Quiet Years Thirty Quiet Years

What ever you think happened at Area 51 dropped from the headlines totally. Actually, the news dropped to the point that very few people thought about this subject for a second up to the point that Stanton Friedman was being interviewed by a radio station local to Baton Rouge. that was located in Baton Rouge, Louisiana. Friedman has earned himself a name as one of the leading authorities on UFOs. When the program was about to end, while Friedman and the station's manager Friedman were discussing, Friedman informed the station manager it was time to interview Jesse Marcel who was living in Louisiana during the time.

It's like what took place in the field a long time ago has been resurfacing on the news. A lot of people believe the incident that occurred on night just a hot air balloon frequently ask what the reasoning behind why no one spoke out for nearly thirty years. The answer is simple as per several of those that were part of the event at the time. According to them, shortly following the incident, they were met by two military officers and were told that if they spoke to them, they'd be shot.

As an example, young mortician Glenn Dennis says that he along with Sheriff Wilcox were in Wilcox's office when two officials from the military came up to the pair. The two men informed the two that if one did not speak about what transpired in the field, then they as well as their families would die.

The daughter of Wilcox who told her daughter that two officials from the military visited their home with huge machine guns is the basis for the story. She claims that she has vivid memories of listening to the officials warn their parents that if they even spoke, they'd be taken from them.

When you ask an officer from the police force They will inform the person engaged in crime tend to make up different accounts of what happened and they'll never fabricate stories about getting threatened by somebody unless the story is actually true.

Furthermore, if you are spending long enough in the area you'll find that the people who were involved ended their relationships with their extended families and claimed that the thing they observed was nothing more than a weather balloon. A lot of them passed away, unwilling to reveal the truth because they were afraid to tell the truth would hurt them.

Chapter 10: The Majestic 12

Whatever side of your opinion about what the military discovered in the fields the day of the incident, a document which many people use to back their argument can be found in that of the Majestic 12 document that says that bodies as well as a crashed UFO were discovered in the fields in Roswell, New Mexico. The report was discovered near the end of a film roll which was handed over by UFO researcher Jaime S. Shandera in 1984. Shandera says that an elite group of insiders had reportedly told Shandera earlier in the day that they would like the truth to be revealed. It's important to keep in mind that this document has not been released to the public. What the public is able to be able to see are photos from the documents.

No matter if you think the authenticity of the document or fake, the researchers have found over 160 witnesses who participated in some aspect of the initial investigation by using the document. They have not provided sufficient evidence to support the idea that the balloon was actually a meteorological one which crashed in the grassland. Furthermore, all of their evidence indicates that there was a crash, and the evidence found by the authorities was an UFO.

Lee Graham, an aerospace worker who was required by law to reveal anything that he observed leaks that stated "Top secret." Therefore He reported the thief and the theft to FBI. After one year of investigations and investigation, the FBI concluded that the files were genuine.

The members of the Majestic 12 committee resemble a list of the top people from the world of science. The chairman of the committee was Dr. Lloyd V. Berkener who was a part of both the

Carnegie Institute and the Weapons Systems Evaluation Group. The committee also included the Dr. Detlev Bronk who served as the president of both Johns Hopkins and Rockefeller Universities and the Dr. Vannevar Bush whose office was the one responsible for the creation of the nuclear bomb James Forrestal who was the first Secretary of Defense, Gordon Gray who was secretary of the Army and the Admiral Roscoe Hillenkoetter and the Dr. Jerome Hunsaker who was the chairman of the National Advisory Committee on Aeronautics as well as the Dr. Donald Menzel who was director of the Harvard College Observatory, General Robert M. Montegue who was in charge of the White Sands Nuclear Research Facility Admiral Sidney Souers who was the director of Central Intelligence which later became the CIA General Nathan Twining who was chairman of the Joint Chiefs of Staff and General Hoyt Vandenburg who served as the Chief of Staff of the Air Force.

Two of them deserve particular mention because of their belief regarding UFOs in that moment. James Forrestal committed suicide by stringing a cord of a coat of his house in his neck when he was hospitalized in Bethesda Naval Hospital. Bethesda Naval Hospital in Washington D.C. He jumped out of an unlocked window on 16 floors before he fell to his death. The estimate is that Forrestal hung in the air for 6 minutes before dying. The day the president Truman and ordered Forrestal to commence the financial support of the Majestic 12. Majestic 12, Forrestal went to a gun store nearby and purchased a firearm which he registered immediately in the hands of police. In the weeks that passed, Forrestal became noticeably distracted according to his team. Forrestal even claimed that his phone at home was tapped, and that his phone was monitored. Then, shortly just before his death Truman had him exiled from his the office, and he was later placed in a hospital with mental issues. There isn't any evidence to prove that the cause of his death was UFO associated, a lot of experts think that he was unable to get from admitting that he had seen UFOs might be a factor. Some believe Forrestal didn't jump into his own death in any way. They think that his suicide was orchestrated by more powerful individuals worried they would be able to prevent Forrestal might reveal the truth. This is a plausible explanation. that this event could be orchestrated as the officer in charge at the hospital took for a break of five minutes when the suicide happened. Further evidence suggests that Forrestal was recognized as an accomplished writer, yet didn't leave any suicide notes.

The third man on the panel that merits special focus is the Admiral Roscoe Hillenkoetter. If aliens indeed were taken captive at Roswell in the manner that some think they were, others believe Hillenkoetter was the one who instructed the aliens to be taken immediately for transport to Bethesda Naval Hospital and the Walter Reed Army Hospital. Is that the reason why the commander of the base quickly set off for Washington D.C. with a parcel tied around his wrist, as reports indicate?

The same time Forrestal was interviewed by Truman It is thought Hillenkoetter claimed that he believed in the flying saucer was authentic. Hillenkoetter believed that attempts to conceal facts from the general people was futile. However, Truman convinced him that the panic that could ensue following the announcement could be such that there was no need to hide the truth.

It is necessary to answer a deeper question on their own. If the object discovered in the field at the time was merely the weather balloon, what is the reason why the leaders take all their time researching that reality?

The Hottel Memo

Leaked memos and suggests it was an official cover-up. It is known by The Hottel Memo it is dated on March 22, 1950 and is from Mr. Guy Hottel to the director of the FBI. Hottel was Director of his department, the Washington D.C. bureau of the FBI. The document is the most read and viewed piece of The Vault papers that the FBI released.

The document Hottel states that he's taken on knowing the existence of flying saucers. Three have been discovered within New Mexico. According to the document, they were approximately 50 feet wide round with high middles. According to the report, each of them had three bodies around three feet tall. The report continues to mention that the animals were dressed in delicate metallic fabric, and each one was outfitted with blackout suit like those used by pilots of test aircraft.

Experts have pointed out three crucial facts to be aware of when studying the memo. One of them is that it was published three years following the time when the wreckage was discovered close to Roswell. Additionally, the report does not mention the Groom's Lake, Roswell or Area 51. Thirdly, it is important to note that the Federal Bureau of Investigation has not had much involvement investigating unidentified flying objects. It's worth noting however that prior to the incident, Director Hoover was able to direct the FBI to conduct an investigation into any credible UFO sightings.

The report does however make clear that the FBI was aware of the UFO. In addition, the report suggests that it is possible that the craft hit the ground because radar systems in the region at that period interfered with UFOs tracking system.

It is important to note that the Hottel Memo is not the sole reference to the incident found in government documents. However, the government hasn't been very open about the incident. Many people have been forced to challenge with the government in order to force them to admit they did not have any details about the event. One of those who was the most determined to gain data included Congressman Schiff who represented in the First Congressional District of New Mexico. The congressman has since died.

Following a thorough inquiry after a thorough investigation, Rep. Schiff declared that he's deeply disappointed with there is a report from the United States' government General Accounting Office states that the majority of the records pertaining to the Roswell Incident have been missing. The reason for this is that they documents should be permanent records which should never have be destroyed. It is the General Accounting Office says that the records were destroyed forty years long ago. Some of the offices in government that Congressman Schiff called included The National Archives, National Personnel Records Center, Department of the Air Force, Department of the Navy, Air Force Safety Agency, Air Force History Support Unit, National Security Agency, Military History Institute, Army Central Security Facility, CIA, FBI and the National Atomic Museum. There is an unanswered question as to which agencies are the only ones, aside from the FBI admitted to having documents from the Hottel Memo that no other official government agency has admitted to possessing any documents regarding the events.

The Project Blue Book that is meant to be the most authoritative UFO source from Wright Air Force Base does contain no reference to the crash that occurred at Roswell. However, it does contain several references to strange lighting in the skies above Roswell. A lot of people believe this to be evidence that the government is hiding something as the event was certainly known about.

In 1995, the government came up with a different explanation within a 1000-page report dubbed the Roswell Report that they continued two years later, with another report they called The Roswell Report The Roswell Report: Case Closed.

There is a reason to question what the reason it took government nearly 50 years to come with a report which did not even appear to be realistic. Instead of just a single balloon, they believed that there was a complete line of weather balloons from an extremely secret project that went down. The report states that the project was referred to as Mogul number 4. There are no official government documents dating back to the date of this report to support this idea. Naturally, there's an absence of government documents that indicate would suggest that a UFO was involved in a crash. Thus, the user has to make their own judgments.

Chapter 11: Kingsman UFO Amazing Trail

If an object smashed into the desert, near Kingsman, Arizona, on May 20, 1953, anyone knew exactly where the path could lead. This included most the time Arthur G. Stansel who has earned a an excellent reputation in the Air Material Command Installations Division which was a an element of the United States government's Office of Special Studies. He was completely focused on his job in the role of one of most renowned experts working on the nuclear weapons of the government. When the phone rang later that evening and the caller was his that night, nobody was more amazed as Mr. Stansel to hear his boss Dr. Eric Wang on the phone. Wang advised Stansel that he needed to be prepared to go to Kingsman at the beginning of the next day. He was scheduled to travel to Kingsman for an investigation into the cause of a crash.

However, who did the man to debate so early? in the morning? Stansel embarked onto a military plane in order to fly to Phoenix. Just after he left Indian Springs Airforce Base Airport, Indian Springs Airforce Base Airport However, Stansel discovered that he had no normal job because the passengers in the aircraft were led by the military police, who advised them to not talk about one another.

After the guys reached Phoenix and were transferred to a vehicle equipped with windows in blackout. The men was apparent for Stansel that they had been circulated around for some time possibly in an attempt to mislead the passengers regarding their precise whereabouts. When they finally arrived at the scene of the crash and were instructed they were not to look at things that didn't relate to their area of expertise or talk to one another. The job of Stansel in this task was to find out the speed and the angle at which the object was coming down.

When Stansel was approaching the object, the photographer quickly discovered that it wasn't a normal military aircraft like he had initially imagined. In reality, it was an oval-shaped object around 30 feet in size. On first inspection, it looked like it was the hue of polished aluminum. In addition, to make it odd, it was equipped with convex surfaces along both sides with a diameter of around 20 feet in size. More amazing for Stansel is that there was no landing equipment.

In the process of working, Stansel quickly discovered that the object had carved through the earth approximately 20 inches deep however, there was zero landing gears, and there were no evidence that the object has slid, even just a slightly. The discovery was a puzzle to Stansel heavily as the object must be traveling with a staggering speed to dig its way through the sand to that depth. Stansel couldn't understand why the object hadn't made even the slightest of tracks of skids.

Even though it was strongly advised not to examine the craft, since it wasn't his expertise however, he could not resist a second glimpse inside the thing. The first thing that caught his eye was the bright light that was in the spacecraft, but the next thing he knew was that it might be a device of Air Force personnel. Air Force.

Then he spotted the object! He was captivated by the four-foot tall object on the floor of the ship which appeared an animal, however it wasn't. Stansel was unaware of the deep brown color of skin evident on the surface of the object. The object's face was astonished to him. an almost human-like appearance. It was dressed in the silver of a suit, and had the skullcap of silver worn on the top of his head.

Stansel couldn't quite grasp what he was experiencing. In all likelihood, he was an expert in science and had to be a believer in the scientific law and other things that seemed to make sense for his mind. In addition, Stansel among the leading experts around the globe in the field of atomic bombs, but was he a nine-year veteran in the work at Wright Air Force Base. Prior to that his graduation, he was awarded his doctorate at North Carolina State University in Diesel Engineering and his first master's degree was in mathematics and Physics. But the things Stansel noticed just didn't make sense for the man.

When he was done with his work after which he was taken away by an official from the military who the initial remarks of Stansel. When he returned to the aircraft, he commenced engaging in a discussion with one of his fellow scientists whom he had met in passing. They were swiftly escorted by military police armed with guns. They told them that they could never converse, and they were told that should they speak the conversation, they'd be faced with severe consequences. The two men boarded the plane, and were seated silently.

Returned to his position at Nevada, Stansel was told to draft a detailed account of his observations which was then presented to his supervisors. It could have been resolved in the event that it wasn't the case of Raymond Fowler who became interested by the incidents of the night. It was discovered that the two were both employed within the same building at Sylvania Electric Systems. They quickly became acquaintances, and shortly Stansel began to tell Fowler about events the two men witnessed nearly 20 years ago while in the desert.

Even though Fowler was able to share certain details about Stansel's activities, he also covered up the specifics of the person Stansel was using his name Fritz Werner, the story could very well ended in the absence of the case of William Steinman who read about the tale. Instead of pursuing Stansel However Steinman decided to begin his inquiry with Stansel's employer doctor Eric Henry Wang.

In the course of the necessary research, Steinman started looking for the specific article in a magazine which included Dr. Wang's death notice, within the archives of libraries of Los Angeles where he resided during the time. Steinman found that the edition in Mechanical Engineering that he was searching for was missing from every one of the libraries in Los Angeles, despite the issues prior to and following its publication present. Then he found an issue of the magazine's article at the Long Beach library. The article only piqued Steinman's curiosity and by the time Steinman was noticing that he may have gotten the attention of the authorities. Steinman says that his cell phone was intercepted, there was a device for location in his car as well as that somebody had altered his email.

Many researchers, particularly those who weren't earning money from their work would have slowed down. However, this was not the case but with Steinman who was pushed to push himself even further. When many told them about the news that his doctor. Wang had passed away and that his wife resided within Albuquerque, New Mexico. He was genuinely thinking about moving straight away to Albuquerque However, it was decided to conduct some research before making a decision.

He learned the fact that Wang had been born in Vienna, Austria, and was awarded an engineering degree by the Technical University of Vienna. It is unclear what Wang accomplished in the years following however by 1943 Wang was professor in the University of Cincinnati, in Ohio in the United States. He remained there for nine years. He also began employed by the Air Force's Wright Air Development Center. The Air Force moved the office that Wang was working to the Kirtland Air Force base Sandia Laboratories complex, he resigned the position of professor and joined the federal government, where he was employed until his death in the year 1960.

The more Steinman discovered his new knowledge, the more interested the man became. So Steinman wrote a letter for Dr. Wang's wife, telling her some of his personal details and asking her to respond to a few questions regarding the life and work of her husband. The request was not answered So the next day Steinman made the decision to contact the widow. The widow informed the man that she had received the letter, however that she turned the letter over to Military Intelligence at Kirtland Air Force Base. In the meantime, Steinman had learned that there was a possibility that Wang had been transferred to Albuquerque to assist in the repair of the plane that was destroyed at Roswell.

Once Mrs. Wang's confidence in her, she inquired what he was aware of about Doctor Wang's involvement with UFOs. The woman claims that Doctor Wang so worried about the destruction of his work, the notes he took were written in his personal German shorthand. However it was confiscated by the government his documents after the time he died and they were kept in a separate space in Kirkland.

Mrs. Wang told him that she couldn't talk to him about anything else via the telephone. As they were wrapping up the conversation after which Mrs. Wang made several revelations to Steinman that had him awestruck. She informed him that the craft weren't made of German origin as it was the common belief which the government attempted to convey to the public back then. The woman also explained to him that Dr. Wang didn't believe they were created by the earth. Then was the shock that really shocked Steinman. The lady. Wang told Steinman that the man needed to study the evidence provided by she had said to him. Henry Kissinger knew about UFOs.

The fact that Steinman was shocked is an understatement. However, Madame. Wang refused to tell Steinman any further.

Dr. Kissinger was among the most powerful people on the planet. He was Secretary of State during the presidency of President Nixon and the presidency of President Reagan. But, the more Steinman considered his knowledge of the events, in the way his knowledge of them and understood them, the more it became apparent to think that Kissinger had some sort of involvement. He was an Nazi refugee and had joined the American Army Counter Intelligence Corps at 24. Then, he earned his degree at Harvard.

The next place he visited was the CIC Interplanetary Phenomenon Unit, part from the Air Force, directly under the command in 1952. There is a reason to wonder if they Air Force did not believe in UFOs, and weren't interested in them, just as they were constantly telling the federal that they had the unit that's sole function was to look into crashes of UFOs. Of course, it was not a minor unit. It had direct contact with General Marshal.

Following his time in the position for approximately nine years Kissinger later went on to lead the Operations Research Office that reported directly to the Joint Chief of Staff where he stayed just one year prior to becoming the Psychological Strategy Board which was shortly renamed as"the Operations Coordinating Board whose job was to execute secret operations across the globe. It appears that Kissinger was a liar by the federal government since, when he was an exile in a Nazi refugee, he was promoted to The National Security Advisor the year 1969 prior to his appointment as Secretary of State by 1973. It is a mystery what the reason was for why the government continued to promote Kissinger. He was so adept at what he was doing or was there something more in the background?

There is a belief Kissinger's efforts were crucial to halting numerous terrorist attacks on our United States, but there people who think that there is other reasons behind it. Consider for an instant is the likelihood of UFOs that crashed into earth from different planets. What would this impact on the quality of your life, specifically in the case of being wealthy and influential? What implications could this impact on the way you stay at the top? Some experts think the consequences could be huge. In the simplest sense, many believe that UFOs must come from a distance so vast that it is impossible to believe that physical laws and Newton's law are true. That, in turn, would be incompatible with everything that science relies on But what if there could be more.

Are you thinking that aliens have weapons they could use in a war against the entire world? Many have gone as the extent of saying the military has to always keep people from being scared of something. When you glance back over the last couple of years, we can see that people were initially taught to fear communism. Then they were urged to be afraid of terrorists, but now they're being conditioned to fear the Taliban. Is the military truly fearful of foreigners?

If Kissinger had signed peace treaties with foreign organizations, did he manage to receive something back? There are some who suggest that we received technologies from alien spacecraft which has led to improvements in our daily lives. Many cite the rapid growth of transistors for an instance. What did Kissinger need to sacrifice in order to obtain the technology. You know what is said, everything in life costs money.

Chapter 12: Cape Girardeau from the Condon Report

Before people ruminated over Kingsman and wondered about what transpired in Roswell the city, there were a few bizarre events in the peaceful farm neighborhood in Cape Girardeau, Missouri. The events on that night in May could not have been discovered if it weren't for the fact that a daughter asked her grandmother who was dying to share the story at her final resting place with her husband at peace, and so huge was the deceit.

The pastor, who was living in the town for two years, had his kids tucked in bed waiting on local news reports to be broadcast on the television when his phone came in. When the call came in did police from the military want to know what the pastor's plans were to go to the location nearby to give last rights and offer prayers for the victims in the accident?

The pastor told the officers that he'd be more than happy to go to the site and offer whatever possible. He never imagined the possibility of finding the things he found in a grassy area that night.

After arriving at the scene the pastor observed things which he'd never witnessed before. There were three bodies in the dirt with a fourth body lying close by according to his wife. The creatures are unlike anything she has ever witnessed. The creatures were around 4 feet tall, and they featured a peculiar brown skin. The report also states that the pastor was praying on each corpse like they were humans. When he was praying for the dead being prayed over, he was watched by a policeman from the military.

While he moved from one body to body He told his wife that he had seen an object that was different from the ones he's observed. The report says that the craft was a circular shape however, it didn't have a landing gear. The report says it had a brushed aluminum hue. Then, he told his wife that he noticed strange images on the boat and witnessed two policemen discussing how the aluminum was thin and yet not able to bend it.

The pastor also offered prayers to his Cape Girardeau Fire department personnel as well as other personnel who were on the scene. He then left for back home. After returning home, the shaking pastor shared with his wife what he observed. The next day it was the time for the military police to be returning to the home of the pastor. They told him they would not allow him to speak a word about the things he saw on the spot.

Milton Keynes UK
Ingram Content Group UK Ltd.
UKHW020651201123
432908UK00019B/2363